02

CAMERA BAG COMPANIONS™

Digital SLR
Expo

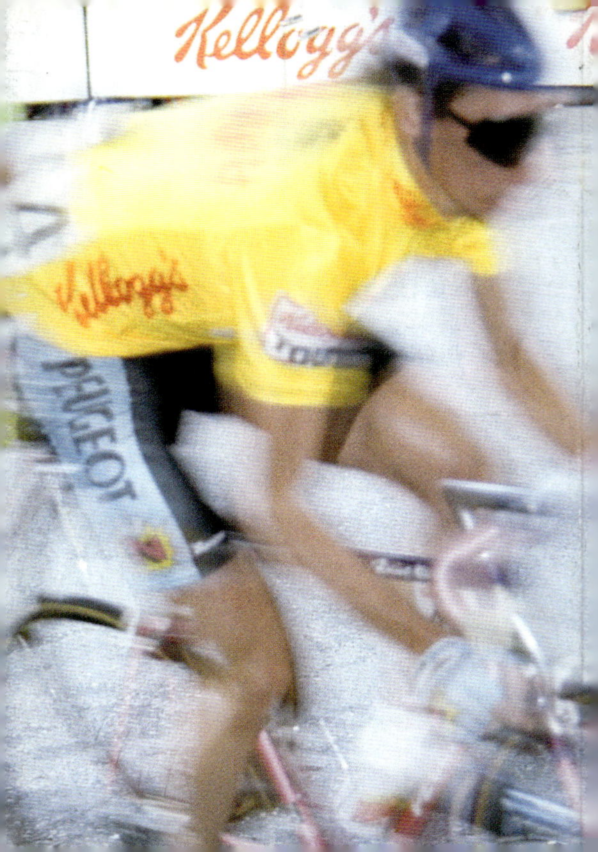
Kellogg's
Kellogg's
PEUGEOT

02

CAMERA BAG COMPANIONS™

Digital SLR Exposure Tips

CIDER MILL PRESS
BOOK PUBLISHERS

CIDER MILL PRESS BOOK PUBLISHERS

Visit us on the web at
www.cidermillpress.com
or write to us at
12 Port Farm Road
Kennebunkport, Maine 04046

The Ilex Press, 210 High Street ,
Lewes, East Sussex, BN7 2NS, UK

www.ilex-press.com

Publisher: Alastair Campbell
Creative Director: Peter Bridgewater
Managing Editor: Chris Gatcum
Editor: Steve Luck
Art Director: Julie Weir
Senior Designer: Emily Harbison
Designer: Ginny Zeal

Library of Congress Cataloging-in-Publication Data:
A catalog record for this book is available from the Library of Congress.

ISBN 978-1-60433-117-2

Printed and bound in China

CONTENTS

What is Exposure?

A camera's sensor needs a certain amount of light in order to capture a photograph—this is known as the exposure. If the sensor receives too much light, the photograph will look too bright (overexposed), not enough light, and the image will be too dark (underexposed).

Because the scenes you want to photograph vary in brightness—depending on the amount of light present—the camera needs a way of controlling how much light reaches the sensor. It uses two controls for this, which work together to regulate how much light reaches the sensor. First, the aperture setting adjusts an opening (the iris) in the lens to vary the amount of light reaching the sensor. Second, the shutter speed controls how long the sensor is exposed to the light.

A third factor is how sensitive the sensor is to light. This is adjustable, and is controlled by the ISO setting. The higher the ISO setting, the more sensitive the sensor is to light.

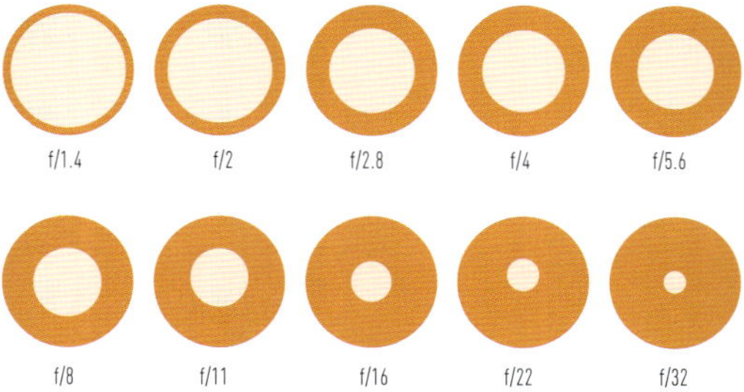

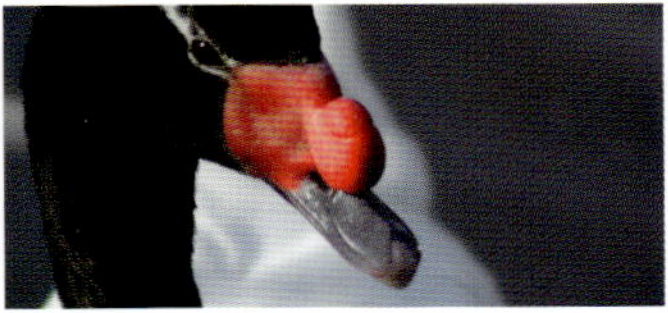

UNDEREXPOSED

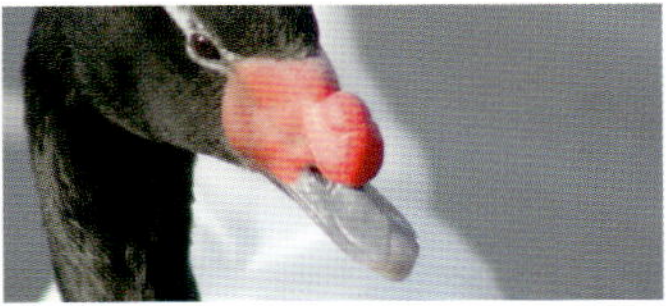

"CORRECT" EXPOSURE

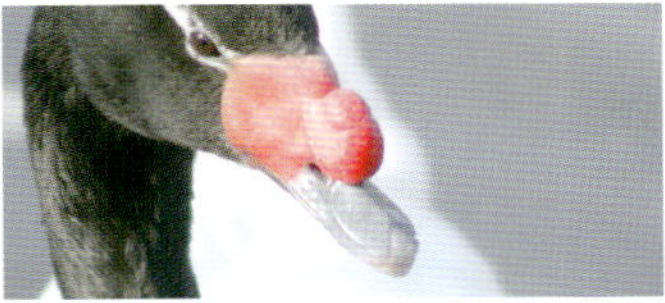

OVEREXPOSED

The size of the lens aperture is measured in f-stops. Each f-number refers to the same amount of light passing through to the sensor, whatever the lens. For example, f/4 on a 35mm lens is actually a smaller aperture than on a 200mm lens because of the different optics, but the exposure would be exactly the same.

A question of compromise

Exposure is complicated by the fact that most scenes are not uniformly lit—in fact, some parts may be considerably brighter than others. Choosing the "right" exposure, therefore, is open to interpretation, depending on which parts you want to show. It's easy to see which of these three shots, for example, provides the best overall exposure. However, the high-contrast subject means that there are parts of the swan that look better in the over and underexposed versions. The red carbuncles above the bill look brigher with underexposure, while overexposure provides better detailing to some parts of the black neck.

Aperture, Shutter, and ISO

Exposure is governed by the three elements discussed earlier—aperture, shutter, and ISO. But what is their relationship to one another? By changing one, how is the other affected?

Let's begin with the relationship between shutter speed and aperture. We know the size of the aperture is measured in f-stops. Shutter speeds are usually measured in fractions of a second. A typical digital SLR will have the following preset options: 1/8000 sec, 1/4000 sec, 1/2000 sec, 1/1000 sec, 1/500 sec, 1/250 sec, 1/125 sec, 1/60 sec, 1/30 sec, 1/15 sec, 1/8 sec, 1/4 sec, 1/2 sec, and 1 sec. Most cameras also feature a range of shutter speeds over 1 sec, up to 30 sec.

Now let's suppose that a particular scene was accurately exposed with the aperture set at f/8 and a shutter speed of 1/125 sec. If you now increased the size of the aperture (a smaller number) to f/5.6—so allowing twice as much light through to the sensor—the image would become overexposed. If, however, at the same time of increasing the aperture, you halved the shutter speed from 1/125 sec to 1/250 sec, the greater amount of light could only strike the sensor for half the time, and once again you would have an accurately exposed image. In this example, therefore, f/8 @ 125 sec and f/5.6 @ 1/250 sec would provide the same exposure. So for any given situation, to maintain an accurate exposure, if you double the aperture you need to halve the shutter speed, and vice versa.

Shutter speed	1/1000	1/500	1/250	1/125	1/60	1/30	1/15
Aperture	f/2.8	f/4	f/8	f/11	f/16	f/22	f/32

The table shows a typical relationship between aperture and shutter speed. With any of these combinations the exposure would be the same.

Shutter speed	1/1000	1/500	1/250	1/125	1/60	1/30	1/15
Aperture	f/2.8	f/4	f/8	f/11	f/16	f/22	f/32
ISO	100	100	100	100	100	100	100

Shutter speed	1/1000	1/500	1/250	1/125	1/60	1/30
Aperture	f/2.8	f/2.8	f/2.8	f/2.8	f/2.8	f/2.8
ISO	100	200	400	800	1600	3200

The tables now include the effect of introducing the ISO setting into the exposure equation. The top table shows the same aperture/shutter speed as the ISO remains a constant. But ,increasing the ISO, while retaining the same shutter speed variables, means the aperture has to stay the same to keep the same exposure value.

ISO sensitivity

How, then, does the ISO sensitivity setting impact on the aperture/shutter speed exposure setting? As briefly touched upon, the ISO setting determines how sensitive the sensor is to light. The higher the ISO number, the more sensitive the sensor, and the more sensitive the sensor, the less light it needs to record an image. Digital SLRs will typically have ISO settings ranging from 100 to 1600 or even 3200 (some go even higher than that).

Let's return to the example opposite. To get the full picture regarding the exposure, we also need to know the ISO setting. If the aperture/shutter exposure combination of f/8 @ 125 sec provided an accurate exposure, we need also to know what the ISO setting was. For the sake of argument let's put the setting at 100. If we now increase the setting to 200—making the sensor twice as sensitive to light—it logically follows that to maintain the same exposure we need to either halve the size of the aperture, or reduce the shutter speed by half. Increasing the ISO to 400, would again require a halving of either the aperture or shutter speed to maintain the same exposure.

Exposure and Shutter Speed

In terms of overall image brightness, any number of aperture/shutter/ISO combinations will produce a well-exposed photograph of any given scene, so why choose one over another?

Being able to select any one of a variety of exposure combinations is the fundamental of photography; and owning a digital SLR allows you to experiment with the options in a way that is simply not possible with most point-and-shoot cameras.

While whichever of the possible combinations you use to capture the scene is unimportant in terms of the overall exposure, the particular choice of shutter speed, aperture, and ISO has other effects on the recorded image, eiher to do with image quality, or how you, the photographer, want to capture or interpret the scene.

Let's start with shutter speed. A slow shutter speed may render moving objects as a blur, so if you want to freeze action, you'll need to select a fast shutter speed. However, occasionally, a little bit of blur can help to create a sense of movement and speed, making for a more evocative image.

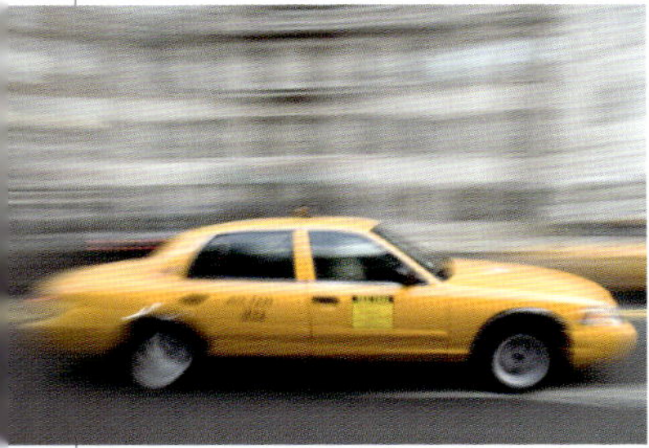

Moving subjects can be portrayed in a variety of ways through careful shutter-speed selection. For example, panning is tracking a moving subject through the viewfinder and then pressing the shutter release during the pan. If the technique is done right, the result is a reasonably sharp subject against a blurred background.

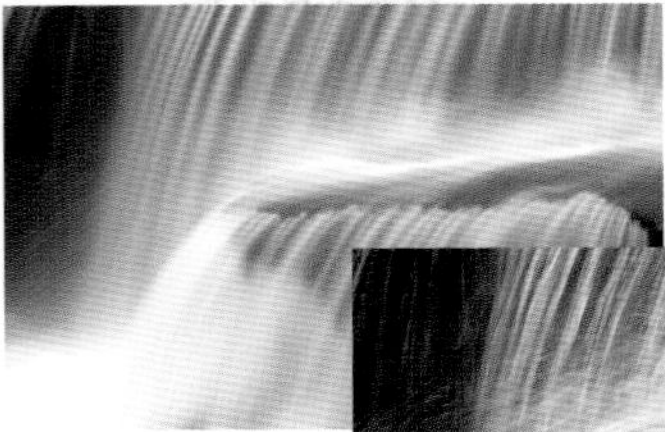

1 SECOND

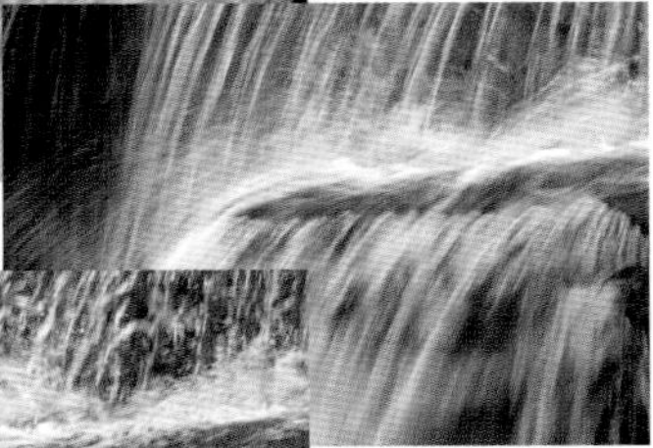

1/15 SEC

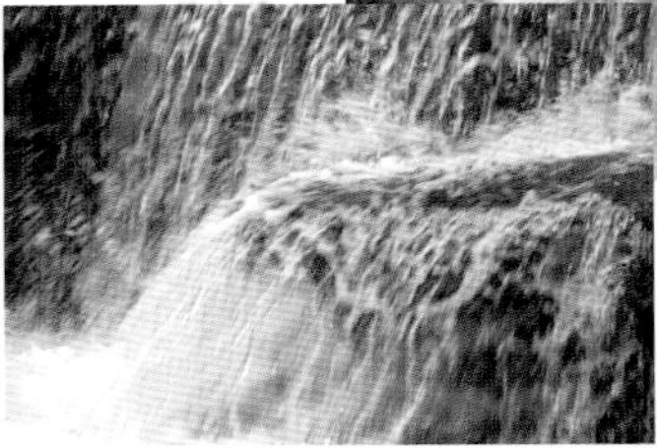

1/60 SEC

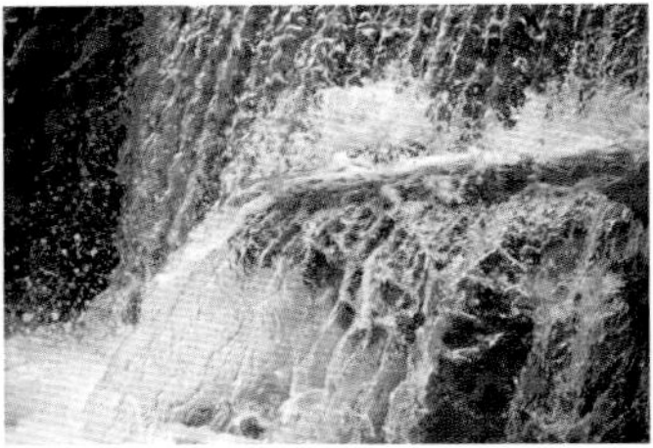

1/125 SEC

Your shutter-speed choice can result in very different interpretations of the same scene. For example, this waterfall cascade was photographed at a selection of speeds. There is no right or wrong approach; it is simply a matter of personal preference and the effect you're trying to create. Any scene that features movement can be approached in this way.

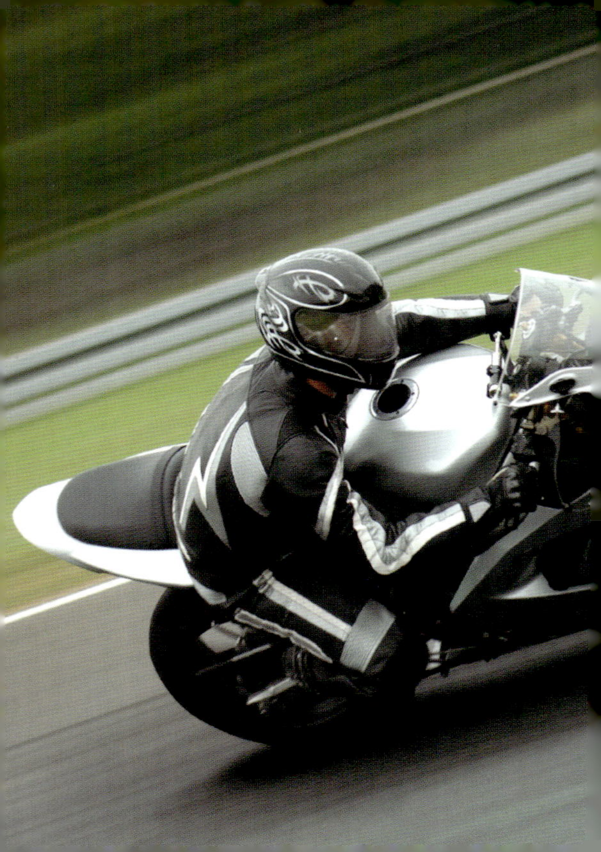

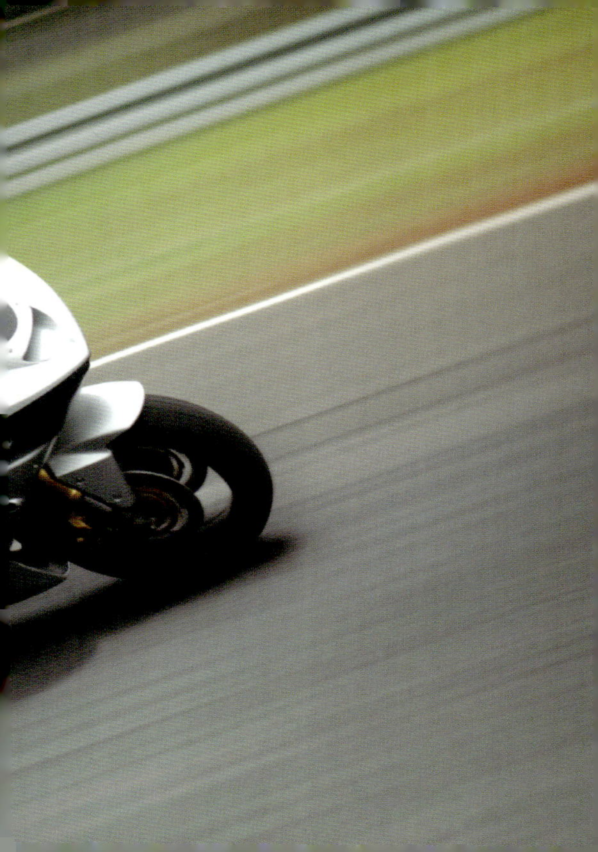

Exposure and Aperture Setting

The aperture setting, as well as controlling how much light reaches the sensor, also governs how much of the scene is in focus when captured on the sensor.

Selecting a wide aperture (small number) makes sure that only a small part of the scene will be in focus—this is referred to as narrow **depth of field**. With a small aperture (big number) much more of the image will be in focus—a wide depth of field. Being able to control depth of field through the aperture setting is another fundamental, creative aspect of photography.

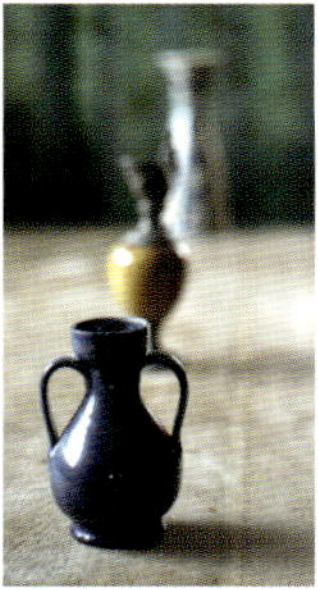

f/2

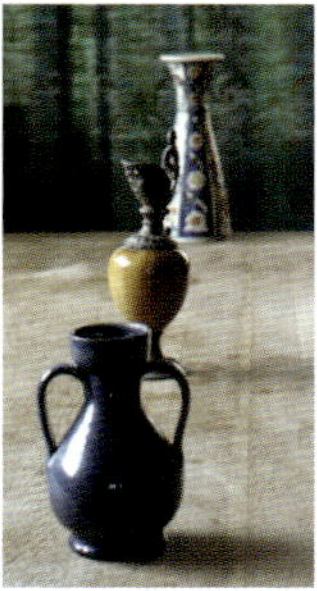

f/5.6

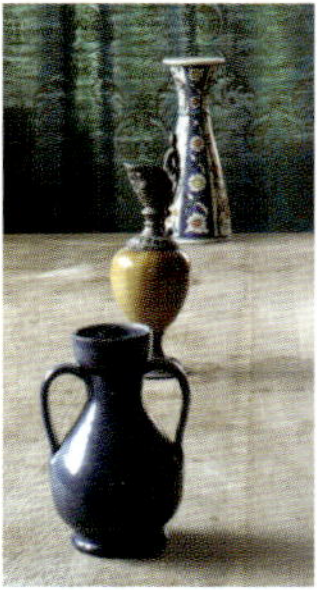

f/22

These three shots clearly demonstrate how the aperture setting controls depth of field (how much of the image is in focus). A standard 50mm lens was used to focus on the first pot. With an aperture of f/2 little other than the front pot is in focus.

Reducing the size of the aperture to f/5.6 results in the second pot coming in to focus, but not quite the last one or the curtains beyond. At f/22 the entire scene is in focus.

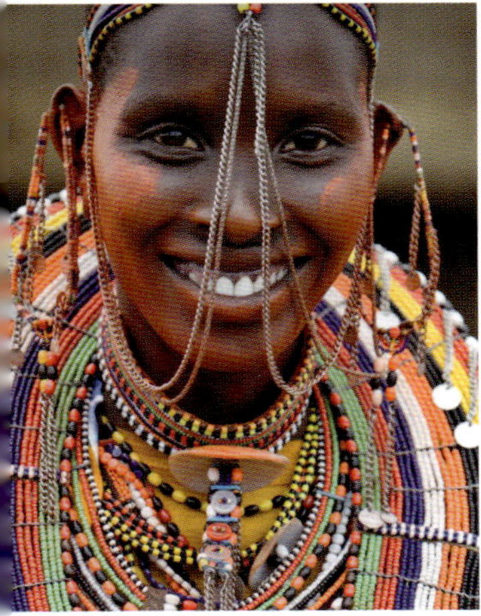

Photographers often exploit the ability to control depth of field when shooting portraits. Here a zoom lens was used in conjunction with a wide aperture to deliberately throw the background out of focus. This technique helps the viewer focus on the subject.

Depth of field

It's not, however, just the aperture setting that determines depth of field. Two other factors come into play, both of which you need to consider when experimenting with aperture settings to control depth of field.

The first is focal length. The longer the focal length the narrower the depth of field. For example, a wide-angle lens of around 28mm will keep much more of the scene in focus than a telephoto lens of 200mm.

The second factor is the focusing distance—the distance between the camera and the subject. The closer the focusing distance the narrower the depth of field.

Maximizing Depth of Field

In certain types of shots, such as a traditional landscapes, for example, your aim will be to get as much of the image in focus as possible. To maximize the depth of field use a wide-angle lens (or the widest focal length setting on a zoom), shoot so that any foreground objects are as far away from the camera as possible, and, finally, choose the narrowest aperture (highest number) that you can. Remember, using a small aperture setting may mean you have to use a slow shutter speed, so watch out for camera shake. Use a tripod or a steady surface if this is likely, or increase the ISO setting.

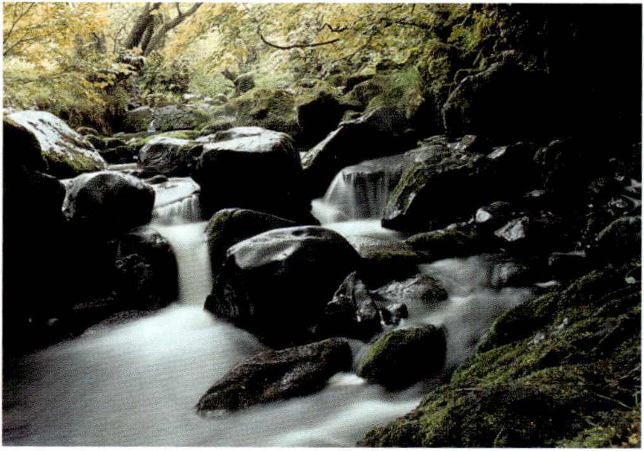

Using efl 20mm and an aperture setting of f/22 helped to make sure everything, from near foreground to the trees in the background, is in focus in this woodland scene. The relatively dark lighting and the small aperture resulted in a lengthy exposure of 30 sec, turning the moving water to a soft foam.

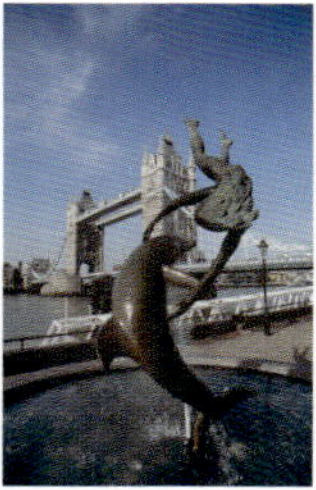

An ultra-wide angle 18mm lens made sure everything was in focus in this scene.

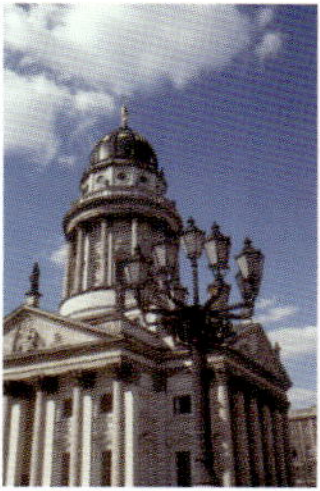

Including something in the foreground helps to add depth to an image.

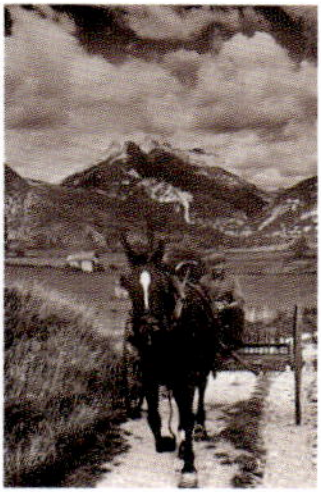

Bright conditions allowed for a small aperture in this shot of a French farmer.

Hyperfocal distance

To obtain maximum depth of field use a wide-angle focal length and switch to manual focus. Instead of focusing on the main subject of your scene, focus just beyond the closest element that you want to appear in focus in the composition. With luck this will be the hyperfocal distance, the point of focus where everything from half that distance to infinity will be sharp. Because modern cameras rarely have depth-of-field scales on the lenses anymore, it's not possible to work out the hyperfocal distance with any certainty, but with a little trial and error you should be able to increase depth.

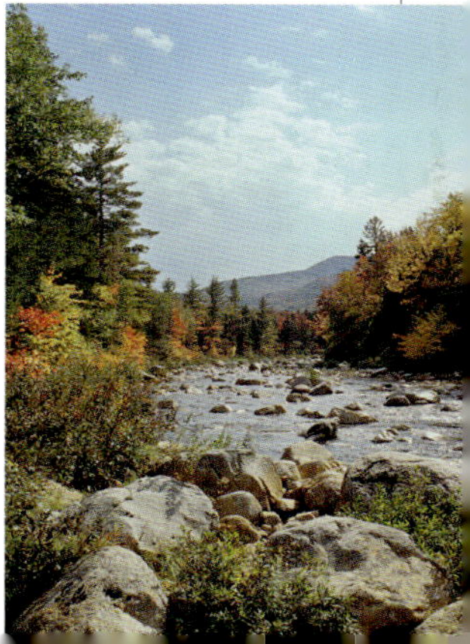

Minimizing Depth of Field

If you're used to a point-and-shoot camera, which, due to their small sensors and short focal length lenses, tend to have very wide depth of field, it might seem a bit strange to actually want to restrict depth of field. But being able to deliberately create a narrow zone of sharpness is one of the most creative aspects of photography. When you selectively focus on the subject, deliberately making sure the background and/or foreground are out of focus, the viewer's eye is instantly drawn to the isolated subject, and, because it's not how our eyes normally register a scene, there is an added impact to the shot.

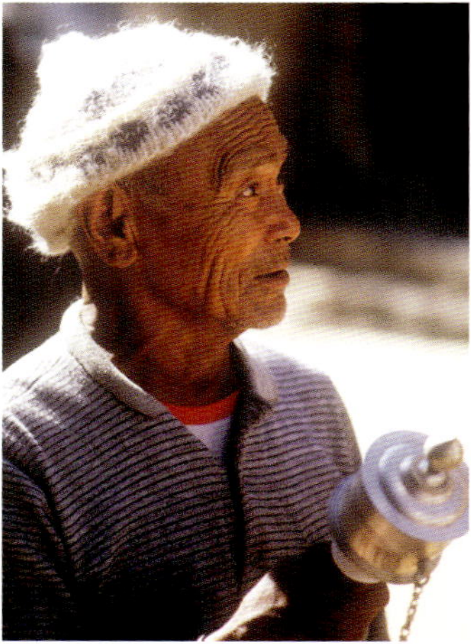

Portraits are an excellent subject in which to restrict depth of field. Using a wide aperture and long focal length helps to isolate the subject from a potentially distracting background.

How to restrict depth of field

There are three key ways in which you can easily minimize depth of field:

- Choose as wide an aperture setting as possible, while still making sure you're obtaining a good exposure.
- Use a telephoto lens or long focal length setting.
- Get as close to the subject as possible. Depth of field decreases the closer the lens is focused.

Getting as close as possible to your subject and selecting a wide aperture setting will restrict you to a very narrow depth of field.

A narrow depth of field is equally effective at blurring unwanted foregrounds as well as backgrounds.

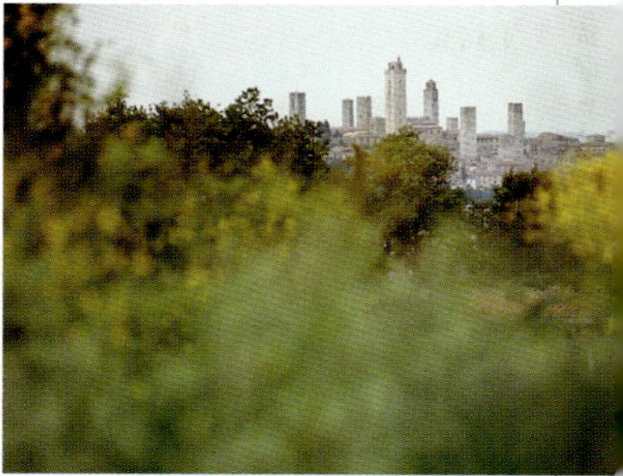

Minimizing depth of field with certain sports photography can help to blur advertising hoardings and spectators. Most sports photography is shot with long telephoto lenses, which helps to isolate the subject.

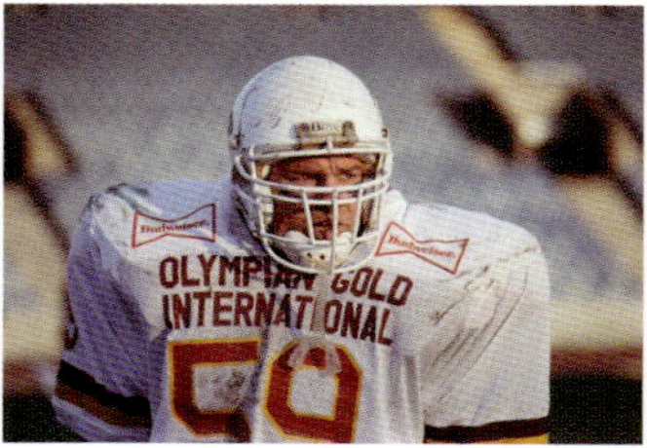

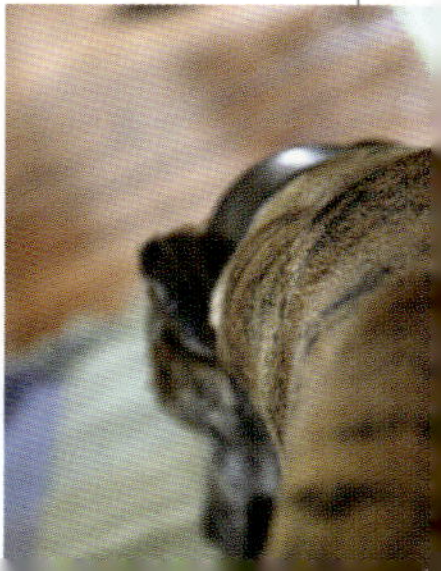

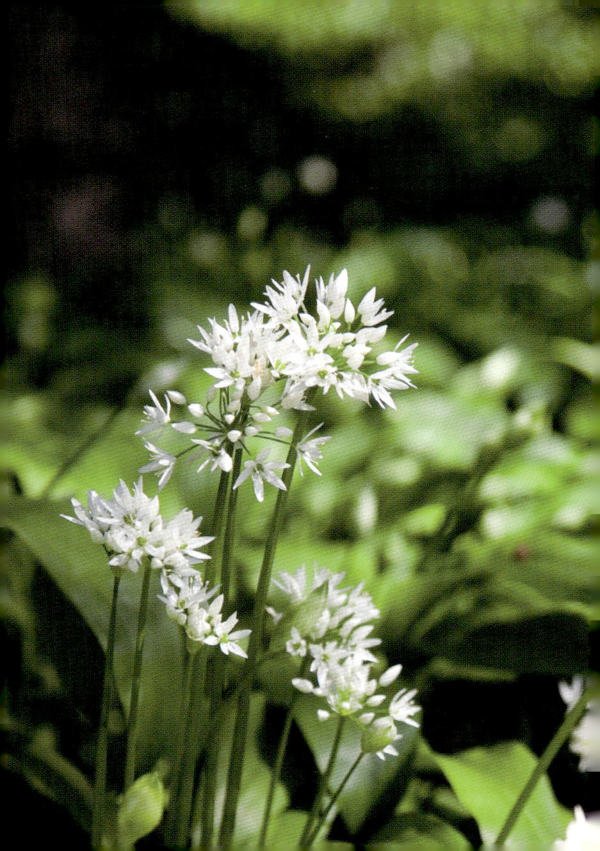

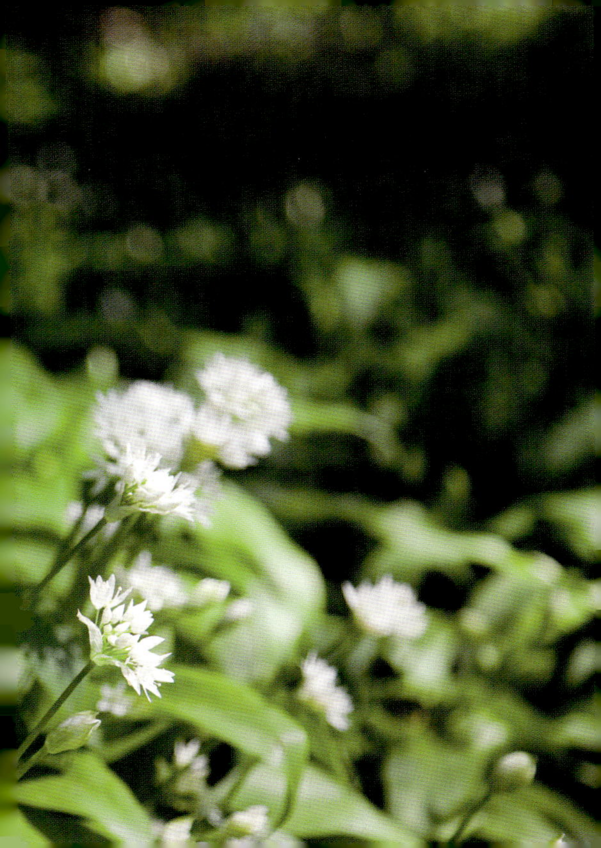

"Stop Down" for Quality

Because of the way they are constructed, lenses will usually provide sharper images at certain aperture settings. At very wide apertures, spherical aberration (in which the rays of light don't all focus accurately to create a perfect focal point) will cause the image to blur, particularly at the edges. As you "stop down" (reduce the size of the aperture) image quality will improve as spherical aberration becomes less of an issue. Continue to stop down, however, and again quality falls off. This is because the light diffracts as it passes through the very narrow aperture—again resulting in a softer image.

Therefore, if the conditions you're shooting under combined with the result you're trying to achieve don't necessitate having to use the widest or narrowest aperture setting then don't; use a mid-sized aperture. Which is the best will depend on your particular lens, but f/8 and f/11 are often regarded as "sweet spots" with standard quality lenses. Set up a controlled test using a tripod, shoot the same scene through each aperture setting, and examine the results at 100 percent on your monitor, paying close attention to the edges of each shot.

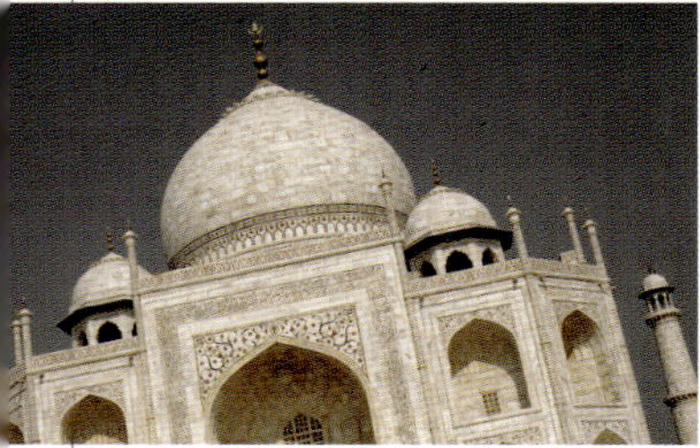

The bright conditions and relatively flat subject being shot some distance away allowed the photographer to use a mid-sized aperture to maximize resolution.

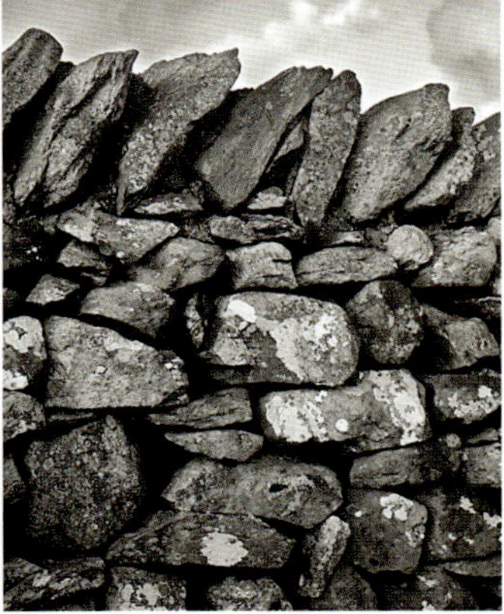

When the subject is more or less parallel to the camera, such as this drystone wall, wide depth of field is not a consideration and so an aperture of f/8 was used.

As depth of field was not important in this telephoto shot of a goat at an agricultural show an aperture of f/8 was used to capture as much detail in the animal's coat as possible.

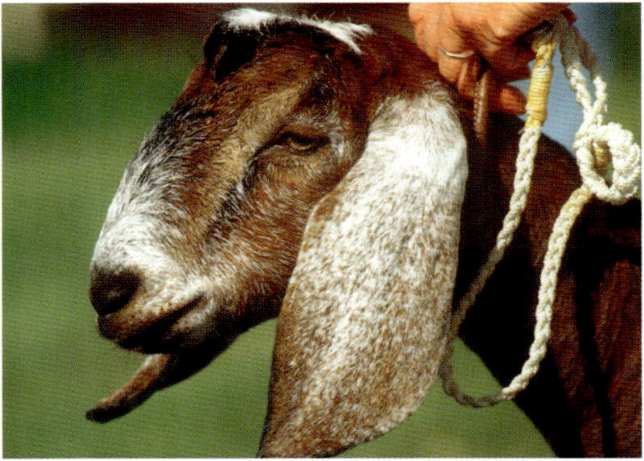

Exposure and ISO

As discussed, the ISO setting determines how sensitive the sensor is to light, and we know that adjusting the ISO setting can be used to alter exposure. Increasing the ISO setting, for example, enables us to use faster shutter speeds, if, for example, we wanted to freeze action, or to avoid camera-shake. Camera-shake occurs when using a shutter speed that is slow enough to detect our own movements as we press the shutter button. To avoid camera shake, the general rule is to use a minimum shutter speed that is the reciprocal of the focal length setting. For example, if you're using a 125 mm lens or zoom setting, the minimum recommended shutter speed is 1/125 sec.

So in very dim lighting, we can increase the ISO setting until we get the desired, fast shutter speed—can't we? Well, in theory, yes, however, increasing the ISO setting increases the electric current in the sensor, which leads to a phenomenon known as "noise." Noise manifests itself in digital images as unattractive clumps of miscolored pixels, most noticeable in areas of even tone. It's often compared with the grain you get with high ISO black and white film, but that's giving noise too much credit. It doesn't have the atmospheric feel of grain, and should generally be avoided.

What's acceptable?

Modern digital SLRs have low-noise sensors compared with point-and-shoot cameras; often noise will be hard to detect up to ISO 400 or even 800 with some models. However, it does depend on the image, and the size of the print. As a general rule, you should use the lowest possible ISO setting that still gives you the shutter speed or aperture you want. However, use a sufficiently high enough ISO setting that will prevent camera-shake, as a noisy image is better than a blurred one. Ideally, in low-light conditions, you should use a tripod and long exposure.

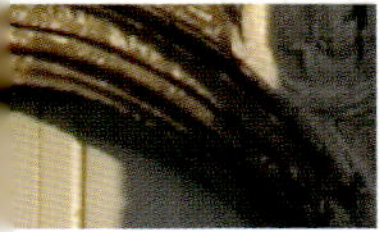

ISO 200 (1/160 SEC)

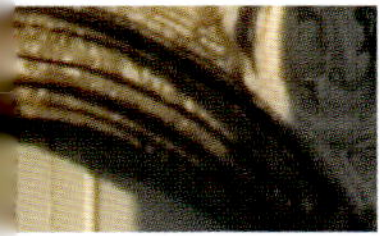

ISO 400 (1/320 SEC)

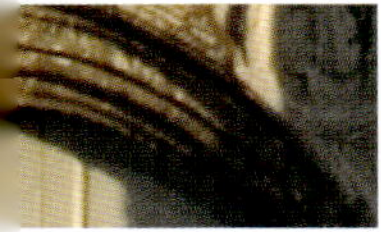

ISO 800 (1/640 SEC)

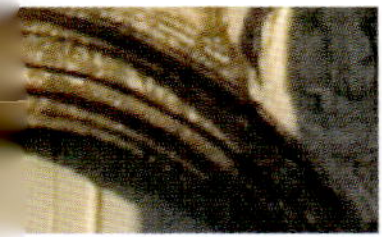

ISO 1600 (1/1250 SEC)

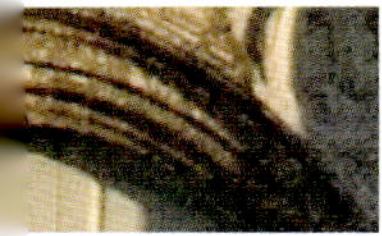

ISO 3200 (1/2500 SEC)

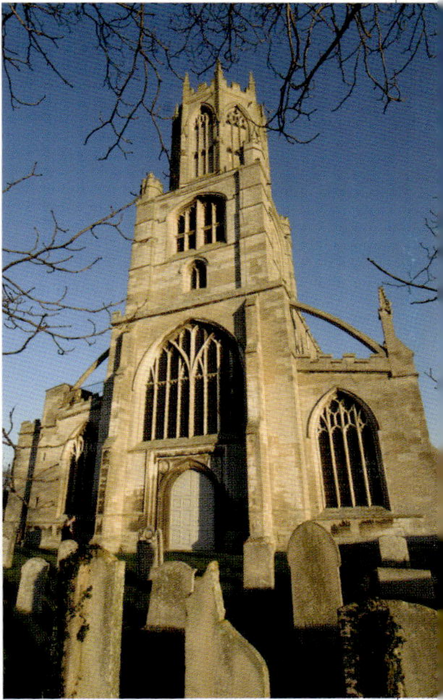

Although increasing the ISO setting will let you use a faster shutter, there is a drawback. This picture was captured at ISO 100 (1/80 sec). A series of increasing ISO values provided faster shutter speeds, but the cost of increasing the level of noise in the picture.

Exposure and Light

Unfortunately, photographers are not necessarily always in a position to choose whatever exposure setting they want in order to create the specific effect they're after—the existing lighting will often come into play. For example, suppose you wanted to capture a glorious landscape sharply in focus from foreground to distant background. To do this you would need a very small aperture (f/22 for example), which lets little light through to the sensor. In low-light conditions, therefore, you would need a very long shutter speed, maybe as long as 1/4 sec or even 1/2 sec. At these speeds you certainly wouldn't be able to hand-hold the camera; so you'd either need to use a tripod to keep the camera steady for the duration of the exposure, or increase the ISO until you reached a shake-free shutter speed; however, we know what increasing ISO can do to image quality.

Alternatively, imagine a scenario in which you want a long exposure of the sea to create a misty, milky effect. However, it's very bright and even with a narrow aperture, you have to use a shutter speed of 1/30 sec to avoid overexposing the shot. In this example, you'd either have to recompose the shot in the hope of finding a darker field of view, or use filters in front of the lens that restrict the amount of light reaching the sensor, so allowing you to use a slower shutter speed.

These are the types of scenario that confront photographers daily, and learning how to work your way around such issues takes experience and technique.

This shot was taken in the late afternoon with low-light levels. It was important to use a narrow aperture to keep the foreground rocks in focus. Fortunately there was a handy rock to rest the camera on to keep it steady during the long exposure. The camera was fired using the self-timer to avoid the risk of camera-shake when pressing the shutter button.

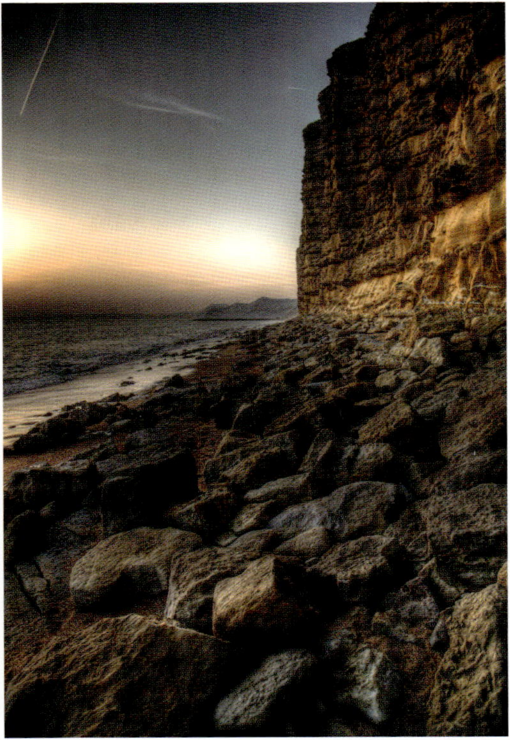

Metering Modes

All digital SLRs have a built-in light meter. This assesses the brightness of the scene to be photographed, and the resulting light reading is used by the camera to set the exposure. Camera manufacturers have worked hard at developing increasingly sophisticated metering systems, or modes, so that exposures are as accurate as possible most of the time. However, because no two scenes are identical, and because the brightness within a scene can vary dramatically from very bright highlights to dark shadows, digital SLRs have different types of metering mode, which vary in the amount of automation they offer to the user.

In general there are three main varieties of metering mode: center-weighted, matrix (or evaluative), and spot. Some makes of camera also offer a fourth mode, partial metering, which in effect is a form of spot metering. Which type of metering you use comes down to the scene being photographed, and how experienced you are at using the three varieties.

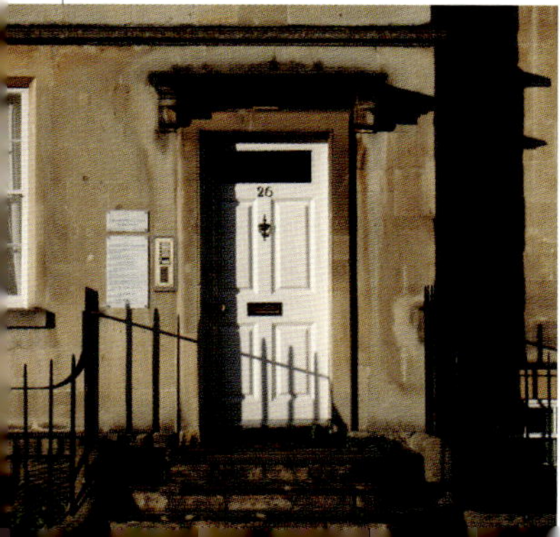

The objects and scenes we like to photograph will often contain a great range of brightness levels. As determining which exposure is "correct" is often a subjective choice, digital SLRs have a variety of metering modes that enable us to control precisely those areas that are accurately exposed and those that are not.

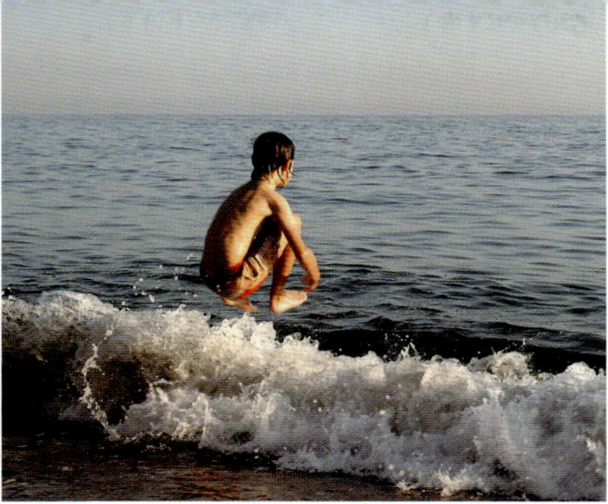

Center-weighted metering has a bias away from a presumed sky. Here center-weighted metering has made sure that the figure is accurately exposed while at the same time holding the highlights in the bright surf.

Center-weighted

The center-weighted metering pattern takes light readings from across the whole image area, but instead of just taking a straight average, it biases the result to the central area of the picture. This, after all, is where the subject probably is, and it gets around the fact that the top half of the picture may well be much brighter than the rest of the scene, because this is where the sky is.
Pros: It is possible to learn and predict when center-weighted metering will get it wrong, and then compensate for error.
Cons: Can be fooled by off-center subjects, by bright- or dark-toned subjects, or by very dark or very bright backgrounds.

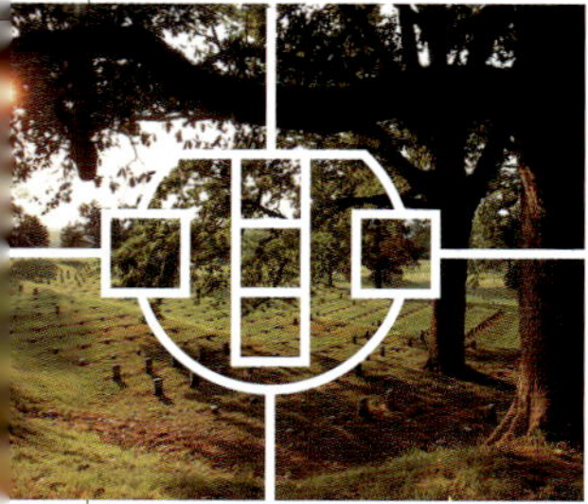

Matrix metering, also known as evaluative or multi-pattern metering, works by segmenting the image area, reading each segment separately, and then comparing the pattern with a "library" of known situations. The overall exposure is adjusted accordingly. Depending on the sophistication of the manufacturer's database of lighting situations, this method is potentially the best at dealing with non-standard scenes, as here, with the sun just shining through the leaves.

Matrix

Also known as evaluative, mulit-pattern, multizone, or intelligent metering, matrix metering takes readings from a number of different zones across the frame. But ,instead of taking an average, or biasing the reading in a predictable way, it tries to interpret the type of picture that you are taking. Using a databank full of typical picture-taking situations and their corresponding light readings, it tries to work out, for instance, whether the background is meant to be black because it is the night sky or simply needs more exposure. Often this kind of metering is linked into the multizone focusing system, so the camera knows which zone the main subject is positioned in.

Pros: More accurate than center-weighted metering, matrix metering is perfect for those who are unlikely to ever manually override the exposure. Is only likely to get the wrong exposure in very dramatic lighting conditions, or when a specific exposure effect is required.

Cons: It's almost impossible to predict when the matrix metering system will get it wrong, and how it will get it wrong, making it difficult to compensate for mistakes.

Spot

A spot meter takes a straight average reading from a small central area of the frame. A photographer typically points the spot meter at a part of the subject and then locks that reading (see autoexposure AE lock, pages 50-51), or calculates an average exposure based on a number of spot readings. Some digital SLRs may have two spot-metering options—a true spot mode that reads perhaps just two percent of the image area, and a partial mode that analyzes eight to ten percent of the image.

Pros: Gives very precise information about brightness values in a scene, and is invaluable in high-contrast scenes, or with subjects dominated by very bright or very dark tones. Digital cameras at least allow you to review the exposure after the shot is taken, so there is minimal risk of getting it wrong.

Cons: You need to know where to point the meter. This system has the most scope for getting the exposure entirely wrong if you meter on an area that is brighter or darker than the ideal average.

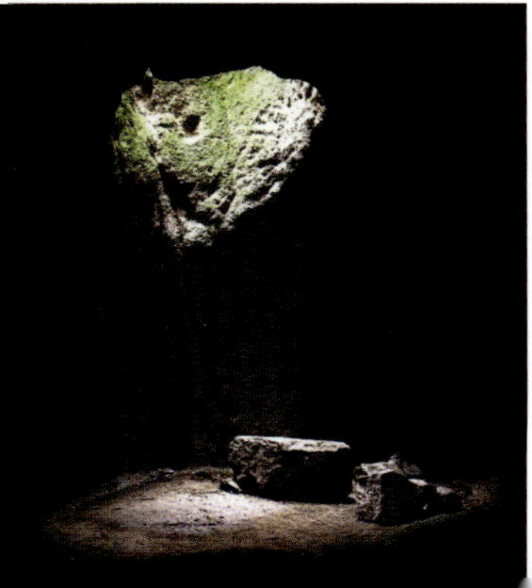

Spot metering is helpful when it's essential to expose accurately for a particular part of an image. In this image of underground caves lit by collapsed ceilings open to the sky, it was important not to overexpose the bright opening. A spot reading was taken from the opening, exposure lock was used to hold the reading, and the image recomposed.

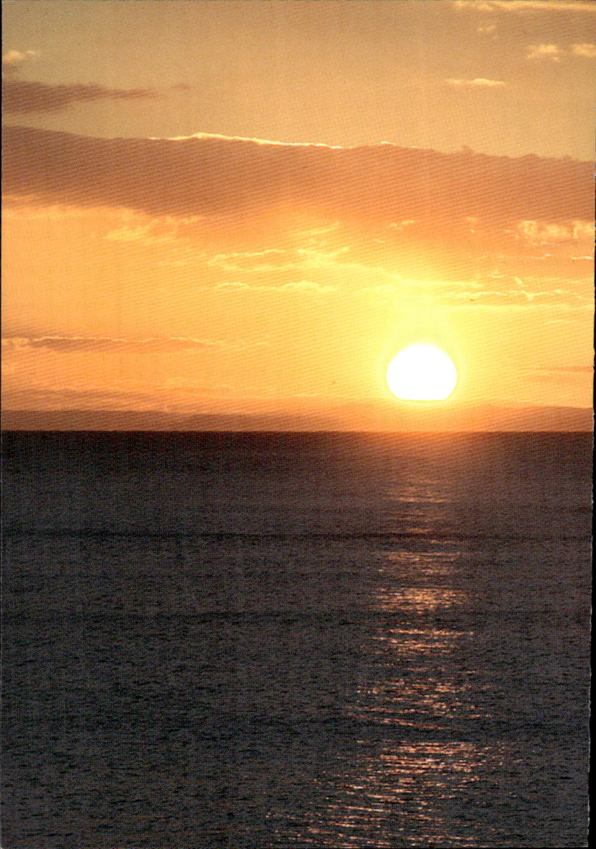

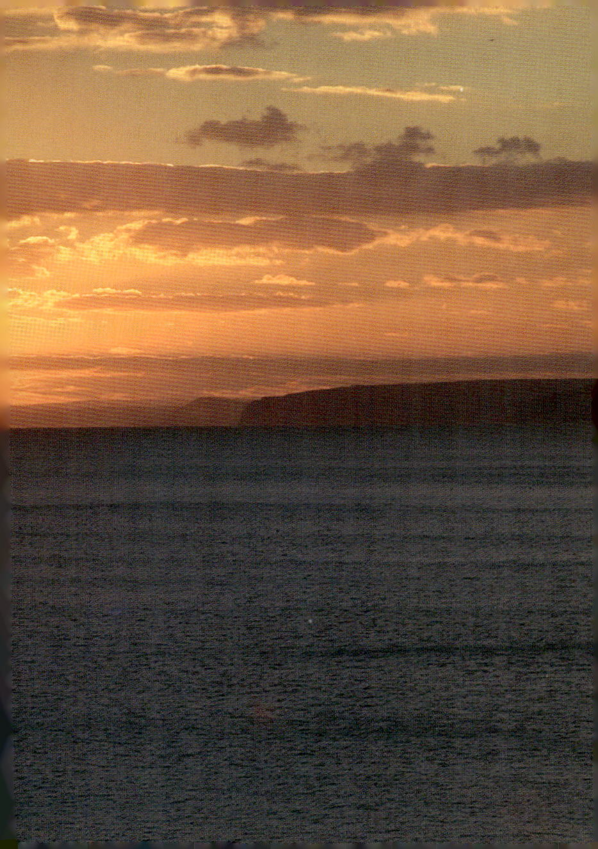

Exposure Modes

All digital SLRs have a number of exposure modes, usually accessed via the exposure mode dial located on the top of the camera. How many specific modes your camera has depends on the make and model, but generally there are two types—subject, or basic, modes and manual/semi-manual, or creative, modes.

The subject modes are intended for the inexperienced photographer and are fully automatic. Relying on the camera's subject modes will provide good results in most cases, but it's important to remember that these automatic settings may not provide the best possible results under all shooting conditions, nor do they allow you to experiment with different combinations of shutter speed and aperture, which is such a crucial aspect to photography. A quick run down of typical subject modes is found on pages 36-39.

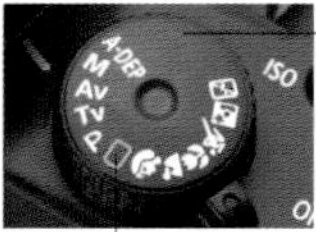

The exposure mode dial from a Canon digital SLR. The subject modes are indicated. As well as setting an exposure suitable for the specific subject, the subject modes also set other parameters, such as ISO and metering settings.

The full Auto mode prepares the camera for point-and-shoot capability. The camera controls exposure, image quality settings, ISO, and so on. As there is nothing for the user to worry about it is convenient, but limiting.

Manual/semi-manual exposure modes

The manual/semi-manual exposure modes are for more experienced photographers who want greater control over the camera's settings. In fact many advanced digital SLRs dispense with the subject modes altogether, as the manufacturers know

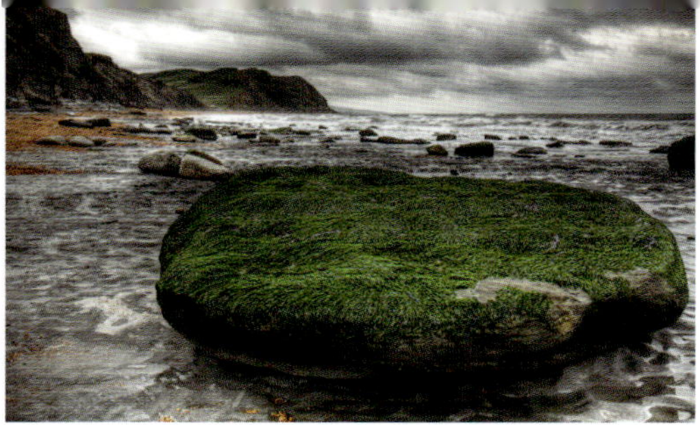

Mastering your camera's semi-manual controls allows you to be much more creative and experimental with your photography. It also means you can take control, when leaving it up to the camera may result in a poorly or inappropriately exposed.

that the users will always want to assume control of the camera, no matter what the subject. There are three semi-manual controls found on all digital SLRs; aperture-priority, shutter-priority, and program/program shift. The fourth creative exposure mode is full manual.

Having increased control can help you obtain a more accurate exposure in difficult lighting conditions or allow you to impose a creative interpretation when capturing a scene. In these modes you also have access to many more of the camera's other settings, such as image quality, file format, drive mode, and much more.

It's important to learn how the manual exposure modes work in order for you to learn how you can improve your photography. Over the next few pages, we'll look in more detail at each of the manual modes and explain how they can be used to obtain more professional-looking results. These modes are covered more fully on pages 40-45.

Subject Modes

Along with the "full auto" setting, there are six commonly used subject modes found on most entry-level and some enthusiast digital SLRs. They may vary slightly in name depending on your particular camera brand, but the function will be more or less the same as described here.

▭ Full Auto

In this mode the camera behaves much like a point-and-shoot model. It takes complete control of the exposure, setting both aperture and shutter speed to achieve an optimal exposure, focuses automatically, sets image size and quality, and the AF (auto focus) mode. This mode is very rarely used by keen photographers as it offers almost no control over either how you interpret the scene or the image-quality settings. The only time it might be useful is when you really have to fire a shot for a once-in-a-lifetime photo, and don't have the chance to check any settings beforehand.

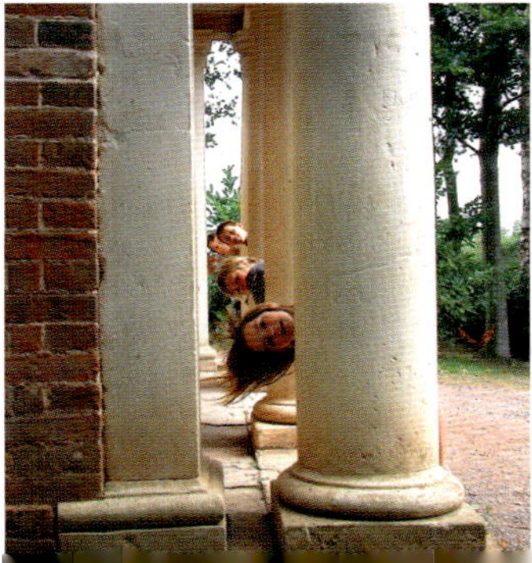

If full Auto, all you need to do is point the camera and shoot; the camera does everything for you, from setting the exposure and focusing the shot, to controlling depth of field and shutter speed.

Portrait

In Portrait mode the camera will select as wide an aperture as possible, while automatically selecting a shutter speed that makes sure of an optimal exposure. A wide aperture (small number) creates a narrow depth of field, so any potentially distracting background will be blurred.

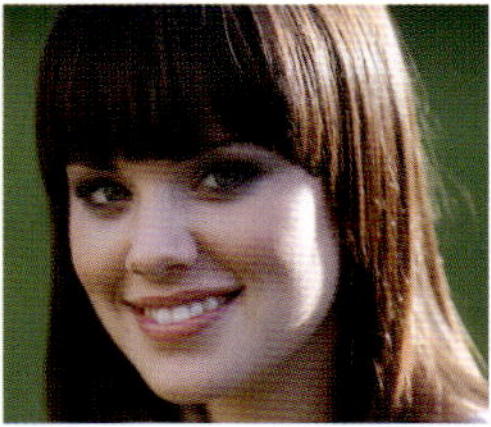

Portraits are most flattering when you use a short telephoto lens or zoom setting, an effective focal length of between 80mm and 100mm is ideal. This also helps blur the background, as will increasing the distance between the subject and background.

Landscape

In Landscape mode the camera will select as narrow an aperture as possible, while automatically selecting a shutter speed that makes sure of an optimal exposure. A narrow aperture (large number) results in a wide depth of field so that as much of the scene as possible is in focus.

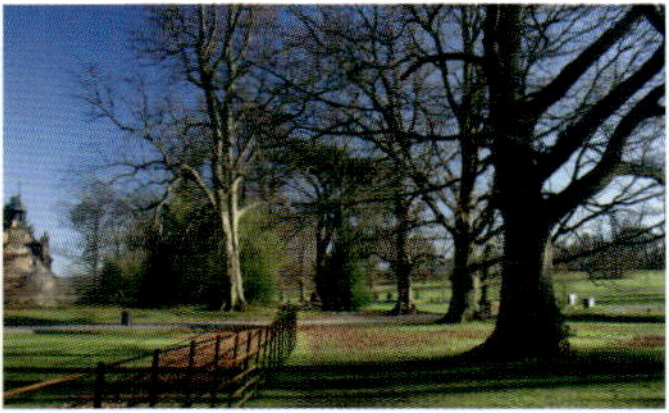

Landscapes are usually most successfully captured using a wide-angle lens or zoom setting; not only will you be able to fit more of the scene into the frame, but more of the image will be in focus.

Close-up/Macro

In this mode, a medium aperture is selected together with an appropriate shutter speed. A medium aperture setting should provide sufficient depth of field to keep the subject in focus from front to back, but leave the background blurred.

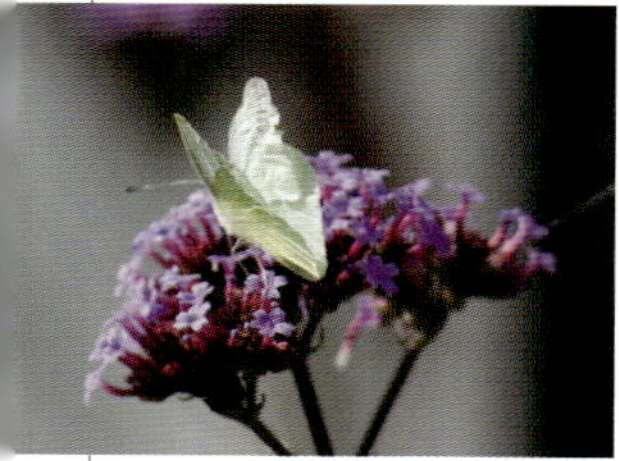

When shooting close-up try to frame your subject against a dark, plain background so that it shows up more clearly. Get as close to the subject as the lens will allow; the minimum focusing distance is usually written on the lens' barrel, such as 0.45m/1.5ft. Any closer and you won't be able to focus on the subject.

Sports/Action

In Sports mode the camera will select as fast a shutter speed as possible while automatically choosing an aperture setting that will provide an optimal exposure. The fast shutter speed is intended to freeze any movement.

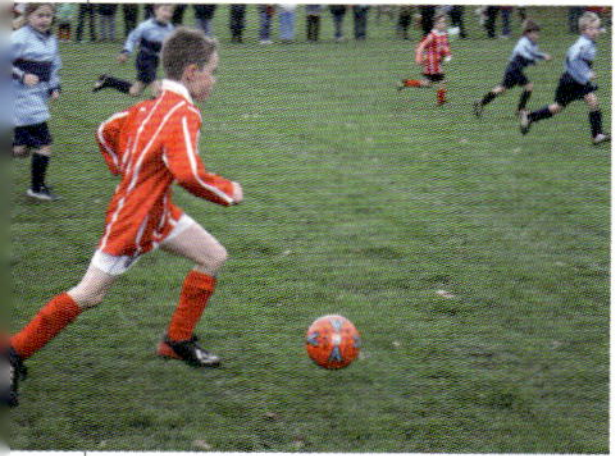

When shooting action, it's best to use a long zoom setting to enable you to get as close to the action as possible. In this mode, focusing will be continuous as soon as you press the shutter button halfway. When you're ready to take the shot, press the shutter all the way down.

Night Portrait

Use this mode for night time portraits in which you wish the background to be visible. In this scene the flash fires in conjunction with slow shutter speeds. Without the slow shutter speed the background would appear too dark. Because a slow shutter speed will be used you'll need to use a tripod, or rest the camera on something sturdy, to avoid a blurred image.

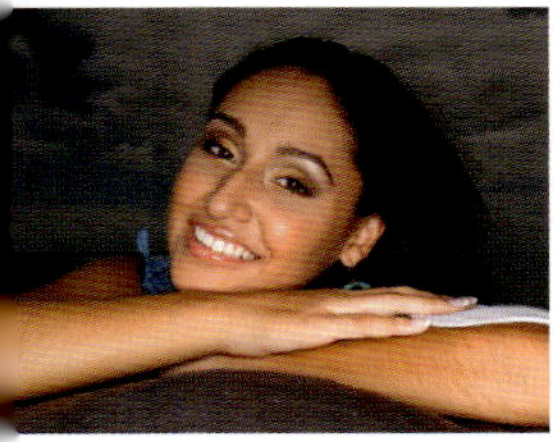

Night time portraits that show the background are best shot with a wide-angle lens or zoom setting to get most of the scene into the frame. Try to make sure the subject is no more than around 5m (16.5ft) from the camera, otherwise the pop-up flash will not light him or her.

Disable Flash

This mode makes sure the pop-up flash doesn't automatically fire in dark situations, in which either flash is not allowed or you want to use a long exposure to capture the ambient light.

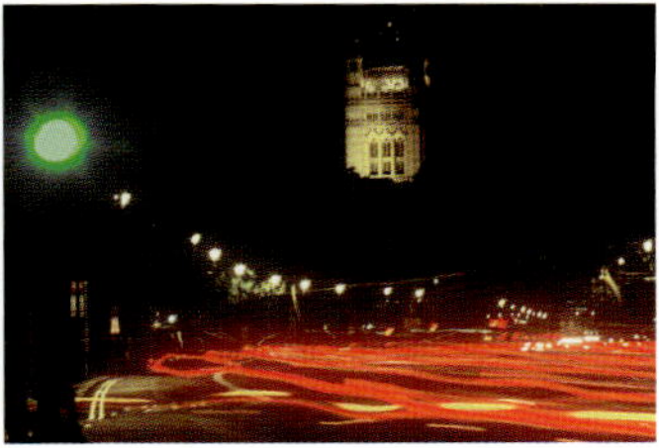

Turning the flash off makes sure that you can take long exposures without the risk of the flash spoiling the exposure or freezing any movement.

Manual/Semi-manual Modes

The manual and semi-manual modes still use the camera's metering system to determine a light reading, but unlike the subject modes, you have the option of taking control of either the shutter or aperture (or both in the case of full manual) and the camera will provide an appropriate exposure—hence the term semi-manual.

Program [P]

Superficially, there appears to be little difference between the full Auto and Program modes. In both modes, the camera automatically sets both the shutter speed and aperture to suit the overall brightness of the scene. However, there are two important differences between the two modes. The first is that with the camera set to Program many of the settings that are locked out in full Auto mode are made available. Depending on your particular camera model, settings that might be made available include: AF (auto focus) mode selection, AF (auto focus) point selection, drive mode selection, ISO speed, metering mode selection, exposure compensation, file format, and white balance selection.

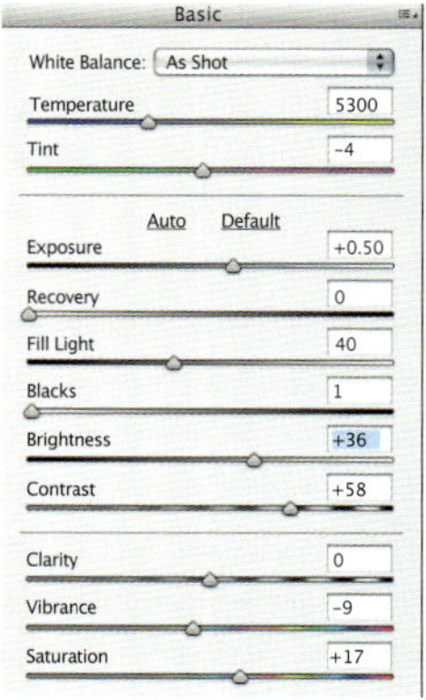

With some cameras, using Program allows you to shoot in Raw. Raw files contain much more information than any other file format, and therefore offer much greater control over image quality during post-production.

Having these additional settings available can make a dramatic difference to the quality of your images.

Program Shift/Flexible Program

The second significant difference is that in Program mode it's possible to change the shutter speed/aperture combination (the program) while maintaining the same exposure value. Known as "program shift" or "flexible program," you can adjust the program by turning a control dial once you have pressed the button halfway to register an initial exposure.

In this way you can, for example, choose to increase the shutter speed—to freeze movement, perhaps—and the camera will automatically increase the size of the aperture to maintain the same exposure. Alternatively you can reduce the size of the aperture (set a larger number) to increase depth of field and the camera will select a longer shutter speed.

Using flexible program is a good way to move on from the subject modes. It affords more exposure choice (and therefore creativity), but the camera will still set a shutter speed/aperture program that will provide an acceptable exposure.

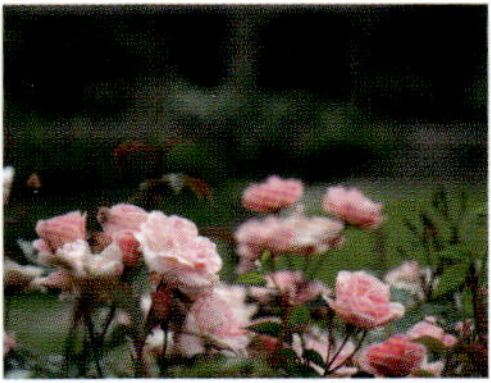

f/4 @ 1/2000 SEC

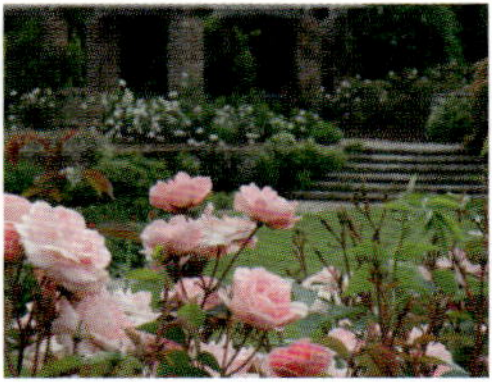

f/22 @ 1/50 SEC

Program shifting allows you to alter the aperture setting, and therefore depth of field, while the camera retains the same exposure.

Shutter Priority [S/Tv]

As its name suggests, in this mode you set the shutter speed and the camera will automatically select an aperture setting based on the brightness of the scene. Having control over the shutter speed is useful in a number of creative ways, but usually you'll find it most helpful when trying either to freeze moving action or deliberately use a slower shutter speed to introduce some creative blur to introduce a sense of movement or speed to the shot.

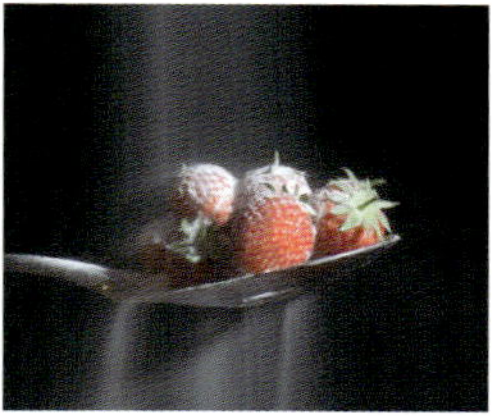

AT A SLOW 1/4 SEC THE SUGAR APPEARS AS A WHITE HAZE.

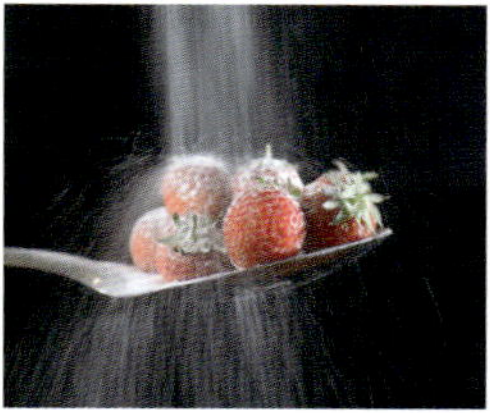

AT 1/45 SEC GRAINS HAVE BECOME INDIVIDUAL LINES OF WHITE.

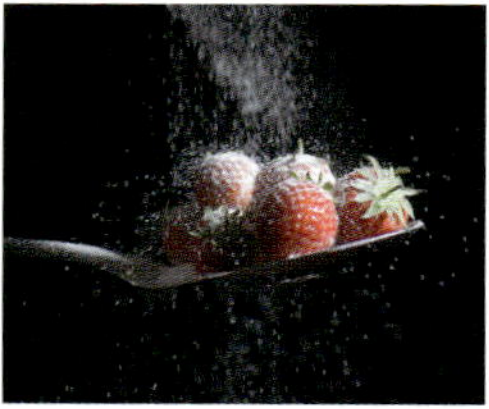

AT 1/750 SEC INDIVIDUAL GRAINS ARE DISCERNIBLE.

Shutter speed is an essential creative control—a different value will often give you a significantly different type of shot. The three shutter speeds here give very different representations.

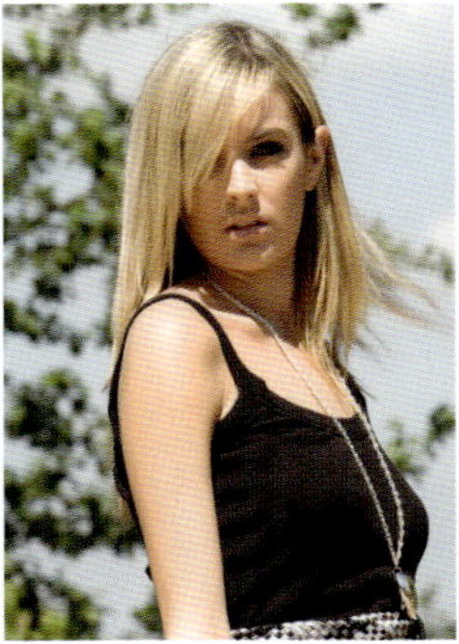

At f/16 the background is blurred but it is still distracting.

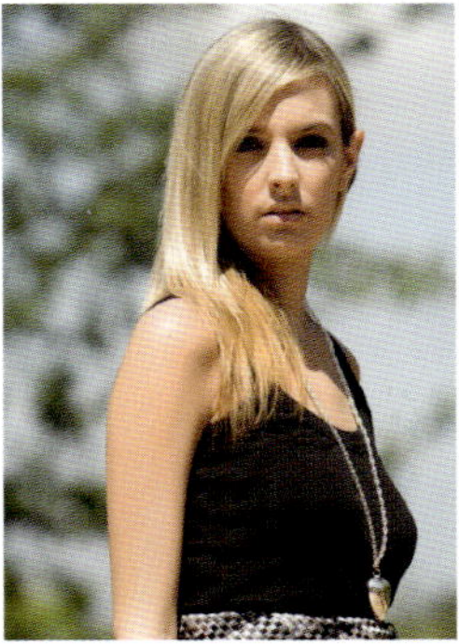

A wider aperture of f/5 has blurred the background so it's less of a distraction.

Aperture Priority [A/Av]

Aperture Priority is used when you want to control the aperture setting, and let the camera set the shutter speed according to the available light. Adjusting the size of the aperture is one of the key ways in which you can control depth of field (how much or how little of the scene is in focus). With a wide aperture setting (small number) less of the scene will be in focus, while with a narrow aperture setting (large number) more of the scene will be in focus. Governing depth of field has innumerable applications, but the most common are in portrait photography, in which a wide aperture setting is used to blur the background, and in landscape photography, in which a narrow aperture setting is used to get as much of the scene in focus as possible. This is exactly what the Portrait and Landscape settings do in the subject modes, but Aperture Priority gives you more control.

Manual [M]

Manual mode offers the greatest degree of control of all the manual/semi-manual exposure modes. In Manual you set both the shutter speed and the aperture, using information from the camera's metering system fed via the exposure level indicator in the viewfinder to determine whether or not you have set an accurate exposure. How you adjust the shutter speed and the aperture settings depends on your particular model of camera, but generally there'll be one dial or control to set the aperture and another to set the shutter speed.

Using Manual mode takes a bit of practice and may well lead to poorly exposed shots initially, but it's an excellent way of learning about the relationship between the shutter speed and aperture settings, and the impact different exposures can have on the same scene.

It's also the most effective way of overriding the camera's own exposure readings if, for example, you wanted to deliberately overexpose or underexpose an image for creative impact.

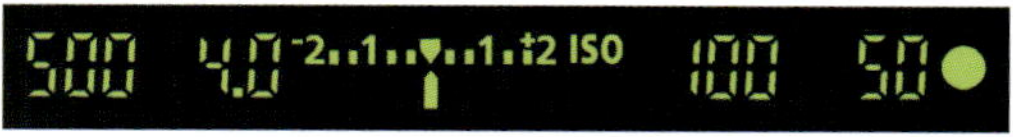

Understanding the exposure level indicator is crucial if you want to achieve accurate exposure in Manual mode. The "ideal" exposure is indicated if the exposure level mark is set in the center of the scale bar. You'll notice that if you adjust either the aperture setting or shutter speed (without changing the view) that the level mark will move either to the left or the right. If the mark moves to the left of center it indicates underexposure, while if it moves to the right, overexposure will result. The further the mark is from the center the greater the degree of under or overexposure, but this does not necessarily mean you'll have an unusable image.

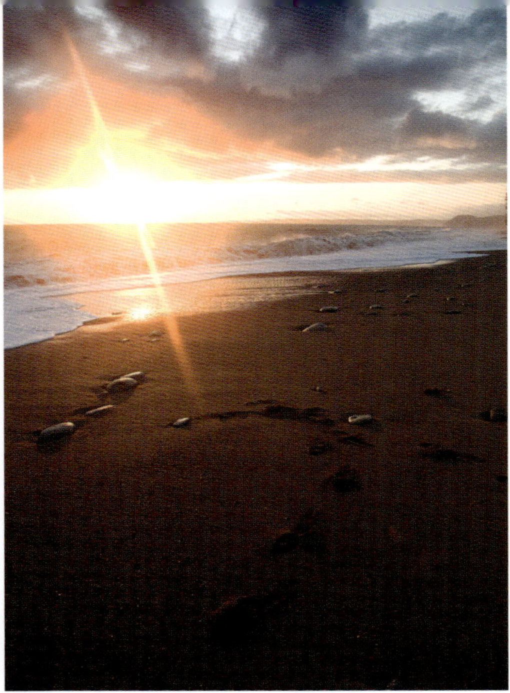

In dramatic and difficult lighing situations, you may find that Manual exposure mode is the only way you can take control of the situation, allowing you to decide which elements of the scene you're happy to leave overexposed and which underexposed. You couldn't do this with Auto.

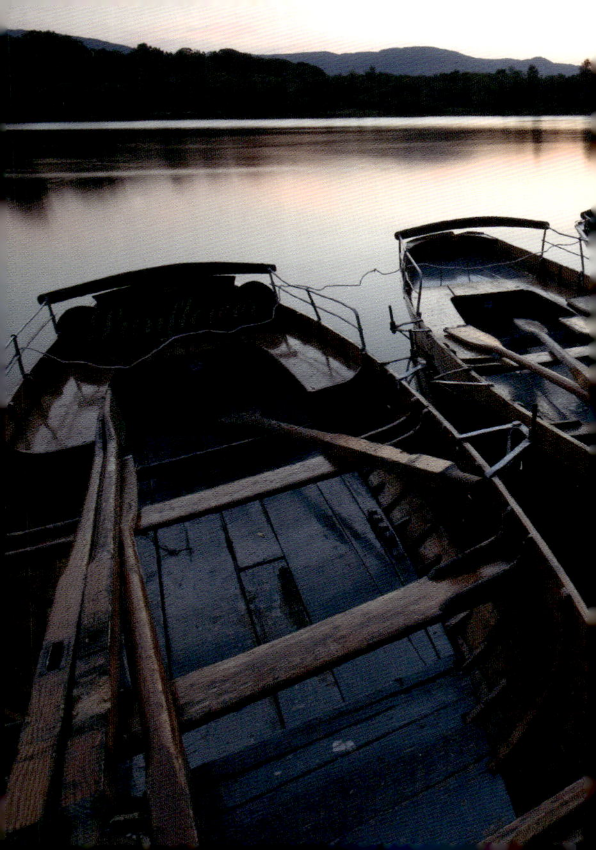

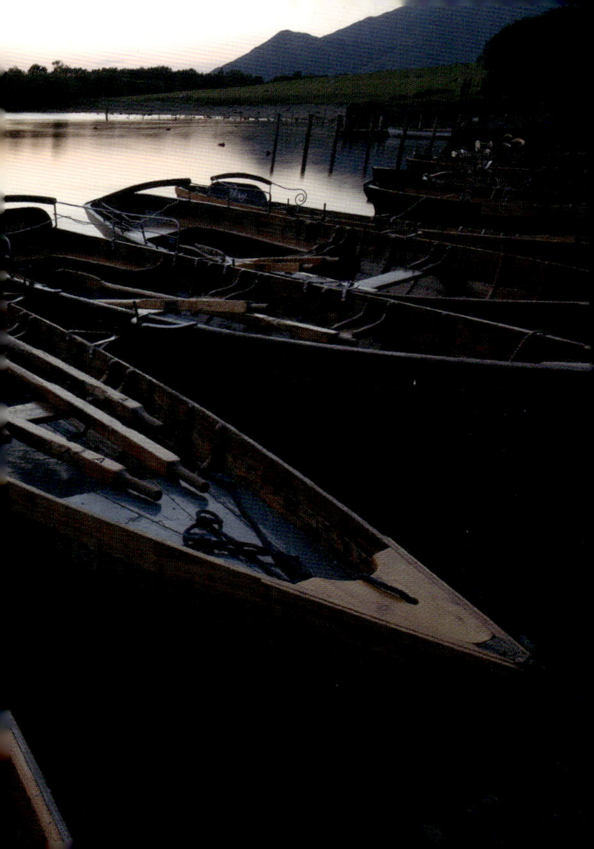

Exposure Compensation [EV/Ev]

Although the camera's built in metering system will usually result in the correct exposure there are occasions when it fails to produce an acceptable result. Difficulties arise when a scene is dominated by light- or dark-toned subjects, resulting in an under or overexposed image.

Problems also arise when there is more contrast in the scene than the sensor can handle. Should the camera save detail in the highlights and let the shadows become too dark or vice versa? This is an aesthetic judgment that you cannot expect the metering system to make and requires exposure compensation.

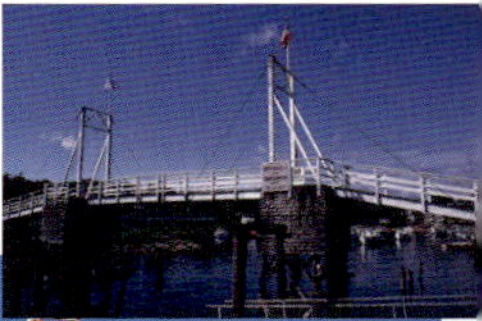

In this typical backlit scene the bright, featureless sky dupes the meter and the subject appears in shadow. Using exposure compensation of +1.5 stops produces a more acceptable result (below).

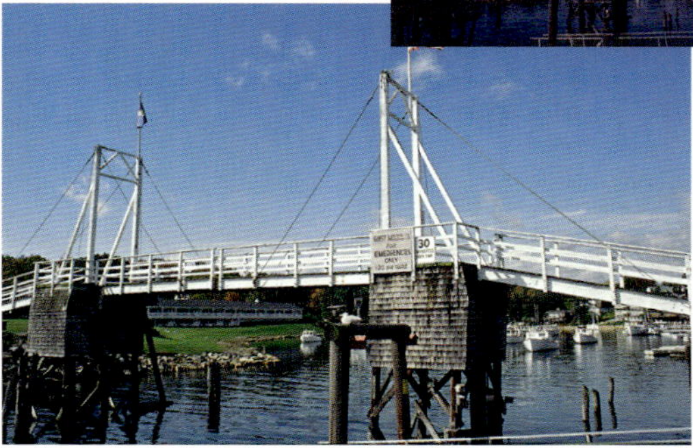

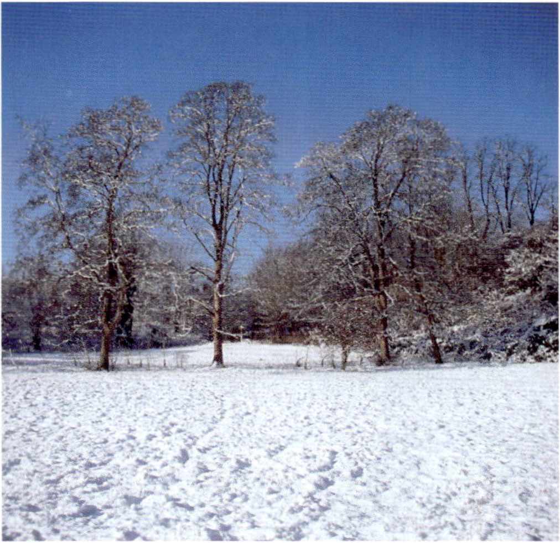

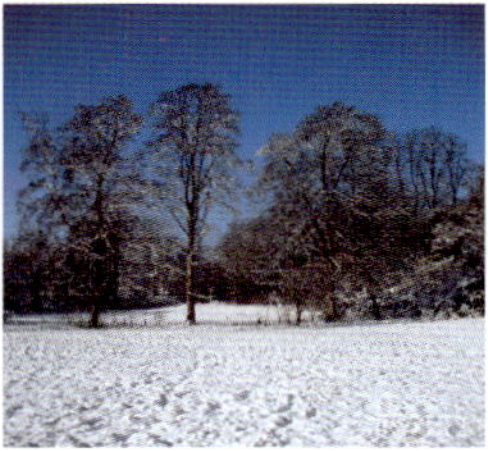

A sunny snowscape creates a bright scene that the camera's meter will underexpose if left uncorrected. Compensating the exposure by + 2 stops (above) creates a more natural looking image.

Exposure Lock

Now and again you'll want to try to photograph someone or something that has bright light behind it, while at the same time recomposing the shot so that the subject is no longer in the center of the frame. Although the camera's metering system will do it's best to resolve the difference in the light on the subject and the brighter light behind it, it will expose for the larger area of bright light and the subject will be underexposed (see below). To remedy this, select the spot or partial metering pattern (see page 31). Focus on the subject in the center of the frame and press the shutter button halfway so the camera takes an exposure reading. Once the reading has been taken, press the exposure

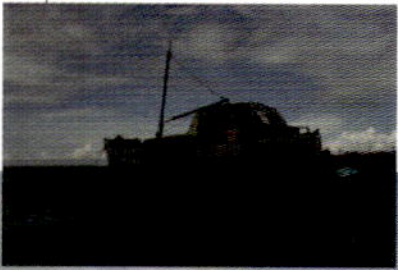

BEFORE EXPOSURE LOCK

Exposure reading taken from boat using spot meter, exposure lock selected, photo recomposed and reshot.

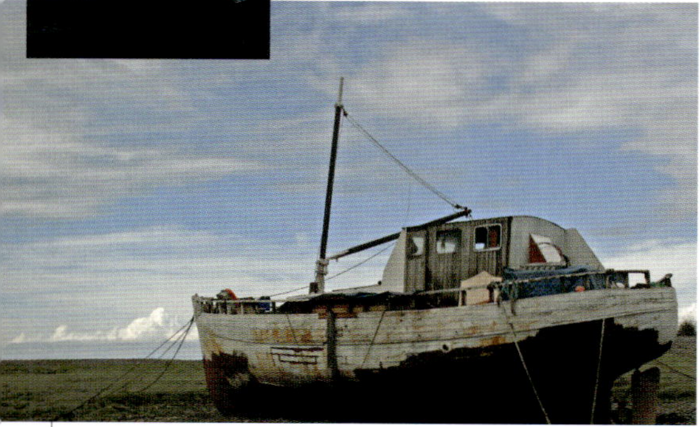

lock button—a symbol will usually appear in the viewfinder to indicate that the exposure has been locked. Recompose the shot and fire the shutter. You'll now find the subject is more accurately exposed.

Exposure lock and panoramas

Exposure lock can also be used to take a series of photographs in which it's important that the same exposure is maintained across the series. When taking individual shots to stitch together to form a single panorama, for example, it's important that the camera doesn't provide different exposures due to variations in the amount of bright sky visible in each individual shot.

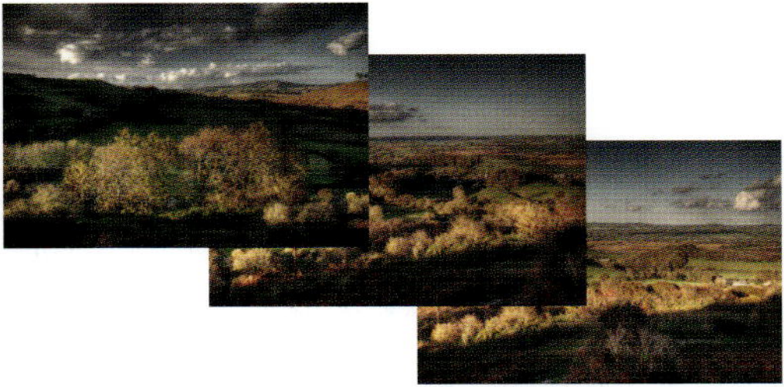

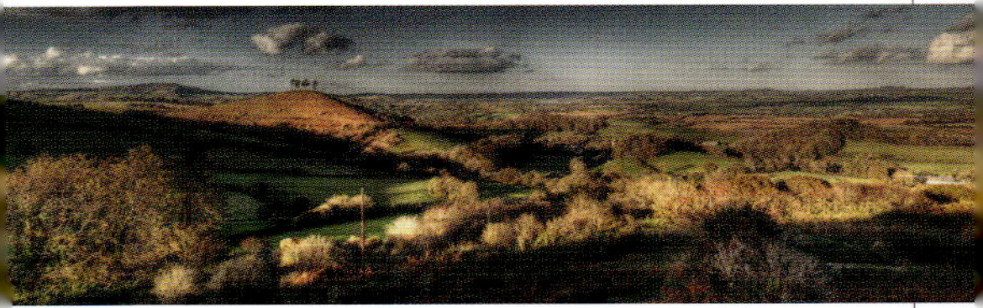

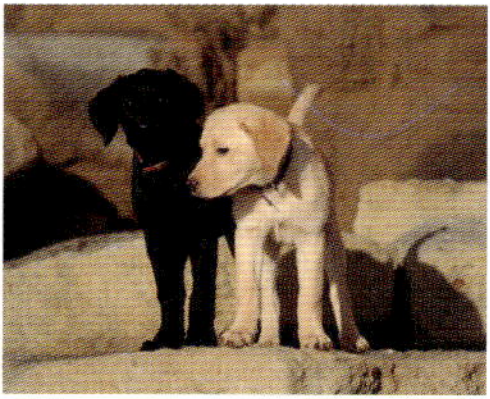

STANDARD EXPOSURE

In this shot, the detail in the black fur of one of the puppies was always going to prove difficult to capture. Bracketing was set to +/–1.5 stops. With the standard exposure, detail is not really apparent in the fur, and so the decreased exposure won't reveal any more. The increased exposure, however, does show detail and provides the best overall result, even though the golden puppy has lost some of her richness of tone.

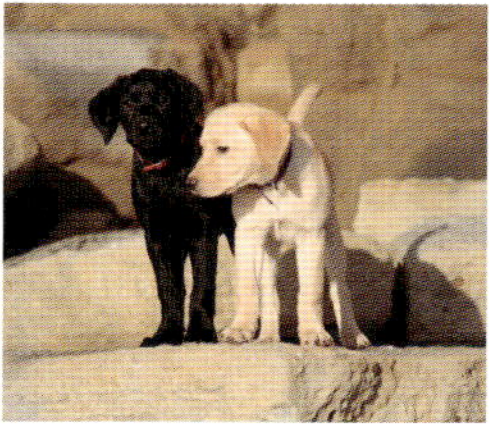

INCREASED EXPOSURE

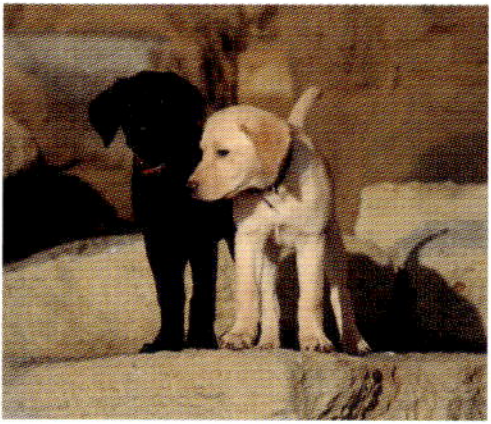

DECREASED EXPOSURE

Bracketing

Bracketing is a way of automatically obtaining a number of different exposures of the same scene in quick succession. In difficult lighting situations having a variety of exposures makes sure that one of them will provide you with the optimum result. How many shots you can bracket depends on your specific make of camera (traditionally it's three), and usually you can select how much you want to increase and decrease exposure (typically up to +/–2 stops, in increments of 1/3 or 1/2 stop). The bracketing settings you select are usually indicated in the viewfinder.

Bracketing and HDR (High Dynamic Range) images

Occasionally you'll be presented with a scene that has very bright highlights and very dark shadows, known as high or wide dynamic range. In extreme circumstances the camera's sensor is unlikely to be able to capture detail in both; you either need to expose for the highlights, in which case the shadows will be underexposed, or expose for the shadows, which will result in overexposed highlights. An HDR image combines exposures that capture highlight detail with those that capture shadow detail. The result, once it has been processed by computer software, is a single image that contains a greater dynamic range than the camera is capable of capturing with one exposure. You can use bracketing to create the various exposures required to capture the full dynamic range (highlights and shadows), which can then be combined in computer to make the HDR image.

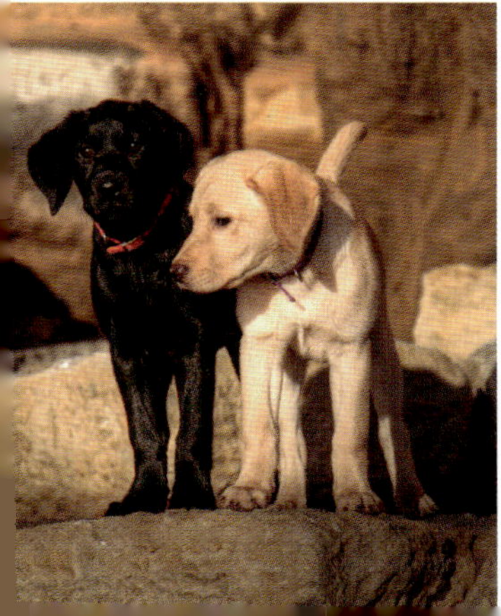

This HDR image was created by combining the three bracketed exposures shown opposite using Photomatix, a popular HDR software program. To make sure the various exposures align properly, ideally you need to use a tripod to hold the camera steady, and hope your subject (if animate) stays still for long enough while the exposures are made. Continuous shooting helped here.

Bulb exposures [B]

Most digital SLRs have set shutter speeds of between 30 seconds to 1/4000 sec (or 1/8000 sec for some models). These shutter speeds work automatically with the metering system to provide accurate exposures across a whole range of lighting situations. However, there is an additional control that operates the shutter, known as "bulb" (B); (accessing bulb varies from camera to camera). With this setting the shutter is operated manually, and will remain open for as long as the shutter button is depressed. Pushing the button will open the shutter, while releasing it closes the shutter. Bulb is usually used when the camera's longest shutter speed is still insufficient to capture enough light for an exposure, such as photographing fireworks, star trails, and lightning.

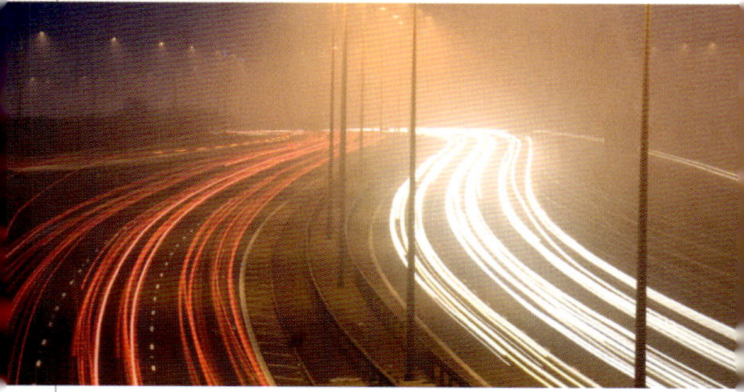

How long you keep the shutter open is a case of trial and error and experience. For car light trails begin with an aperture of f/8 for 40 seconds.

Tripod

Because exposures with bulb are always lengthy, it's vital that the camera is attached to a tripod or at the very least placed on a stable support. In addition, to avoid camera shake and for the sake of convenience, bulb exposures are usually made with a remote shutter release. There are a number of these available for all digital SLRs, some work wirelessly others are attached to the camera via a cable. They usually have a form of "lock" which saves you having to hold down a button for the duration of the exposure. Finally, as noise is more apparent with long exposures, particularly in dark regions, use ISO 100 and experiment with the noise reduction setting if your camera has one. It may produce smoother images.

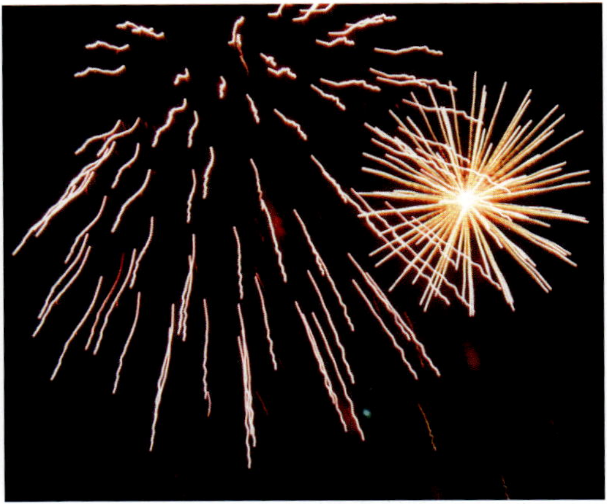

Using bulb to photograph fireworks will usually provide the best results. Open the shutter (using a remote shutter release) just as the firework is about to explode, and keep it open until the firework fades. Experiment by capturing two or three explosions.

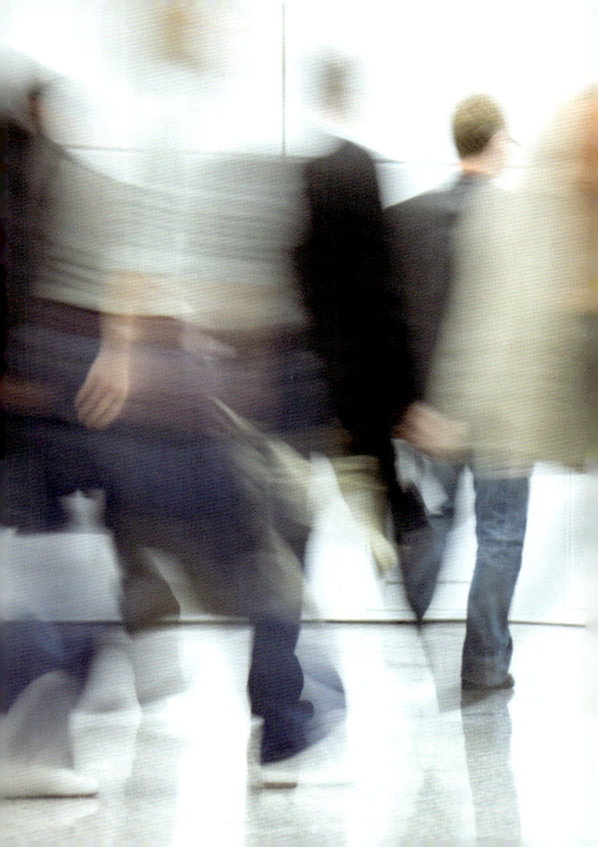

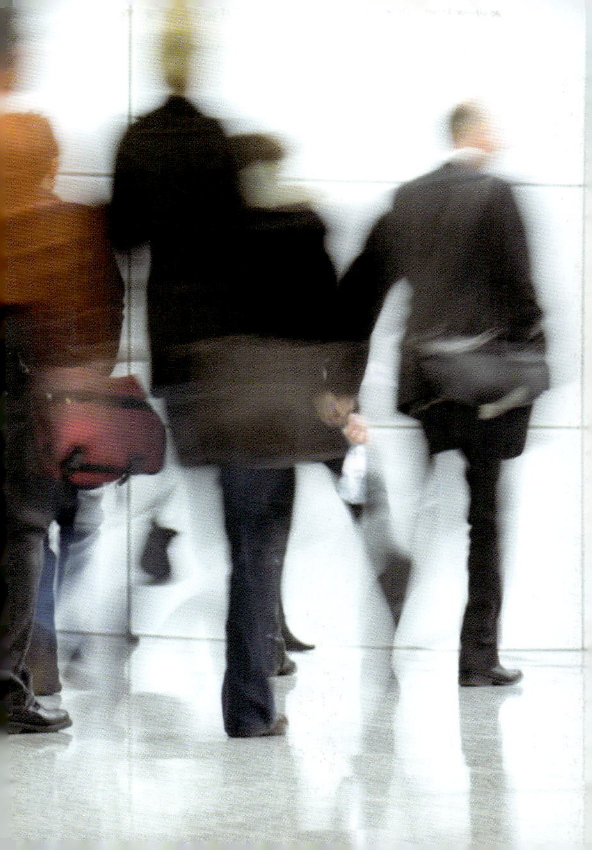

Natural Light

Unless you're exclusively interested in studio work, the vast majority of your photographs will be taken under natural lighting conditions, the sole source of which is the sun. However, the sun's movement across the sky, from dawn to dusk, combined with innumerable atmospheric variables, creates an infinite range of lighting conditions. Over the next few pages we'll look at the impact that time of day and the position of the sun in relation to the subject can have on your images.

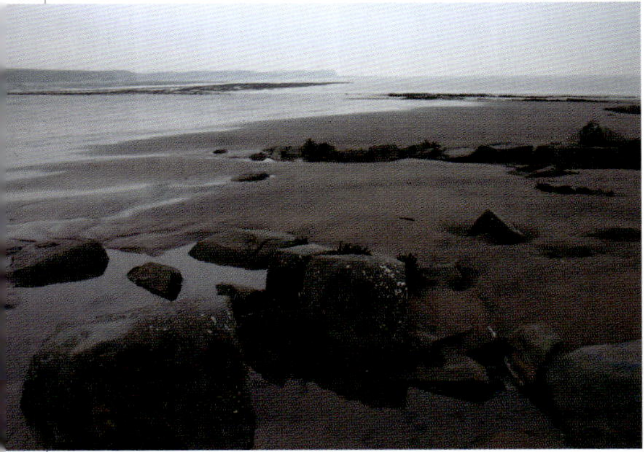

Both of these images show coastal scenes and both are lit entirely by the natural light of the sun, but their appearance and the emotions they evoke couldn't be more different. The difference in location, time of year, time of day, and atmospheric conditions are responsible for the gulf in their visual qualities.

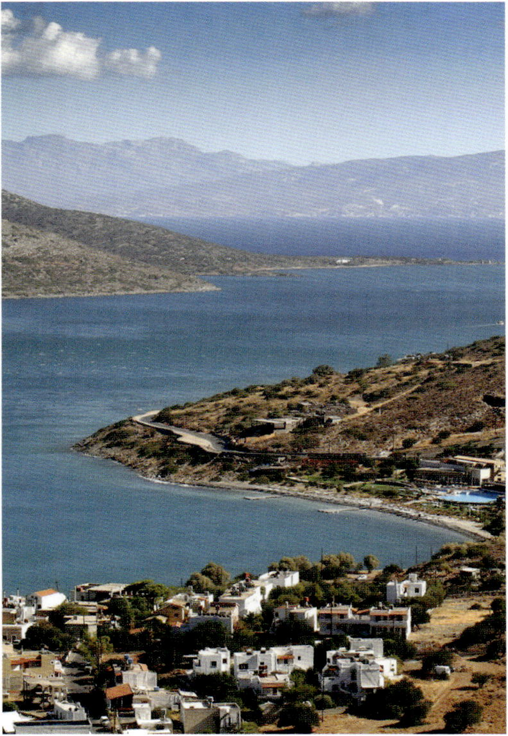

Changing Light

The most obvious variable in natural lighting is the position of the sun in the sky. This changes not only during the course of a day, but is also governed by season and latitude. Equally important is the angle of the sun relative to the subject, and most significantly in terms of your control, the angle of the camera in relation to the sun.

The angle at which sunlight strikes an object has a profound effect on its appearance, most notably in terms of shape, form, and texture, while the natural color of light also changes as the day unfolds.

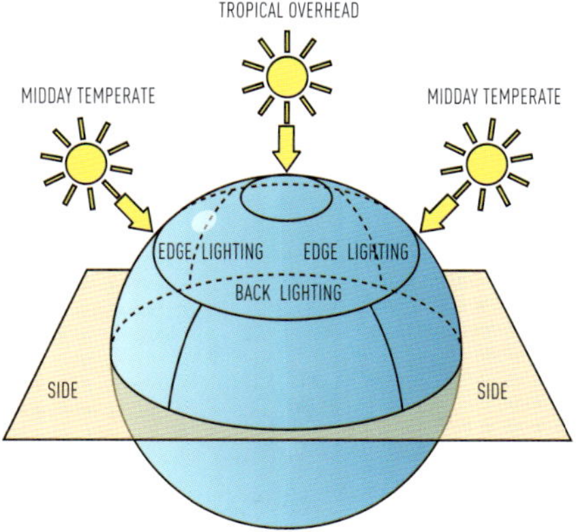

The direction of light, which outdoors can be from anywhere above the horizon, can be grouped together into zones. This "lighting sphere" is segmented to show the main directions, which are dealt with in greater detail over the coming pages.

This series of images shows how a scene can be transformed as the sun moves across the sky during the course of a day.

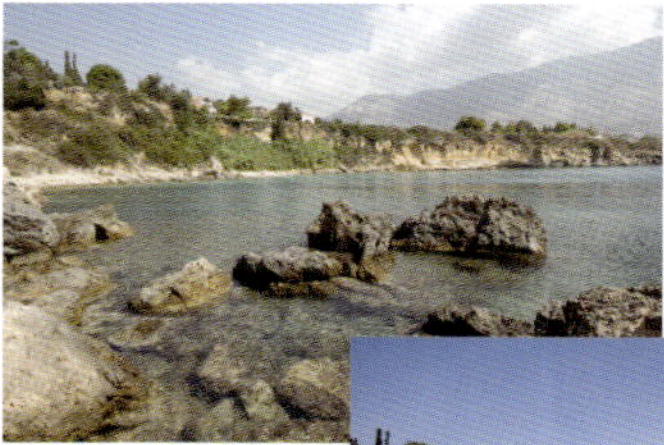

9.00 AM

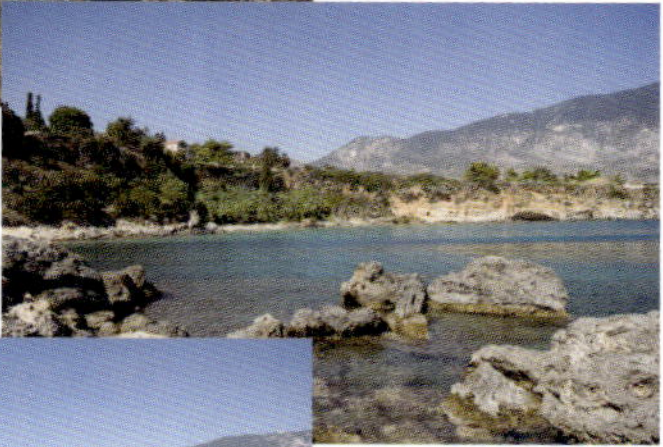

12.00 PM

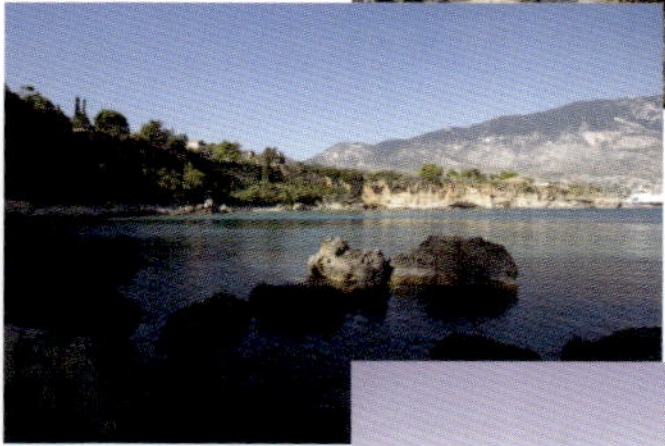

3.00 PM

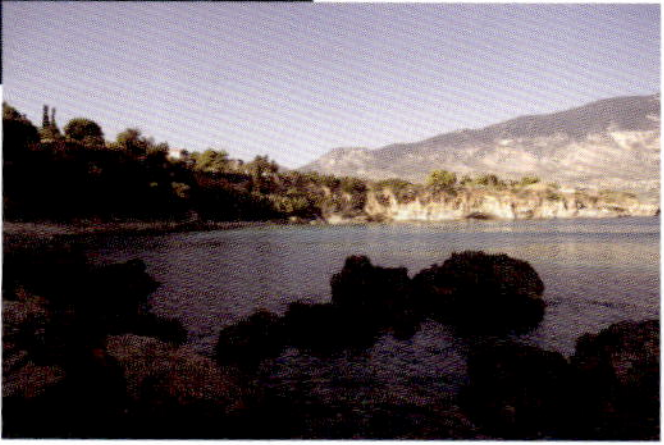

6.00 PM

Twilight

Twilight is the light that is found in the sky either between night and sunrise, or sunset and night. The subtle diffusion of sunlight through the atmosphere is uniquely delicate, and can create very atmospheric images. Photos captured at twilight are usually most successful in a clear sky, when the subtle shading visible in the sky is shown at its best.

With light levels are as low as they are during twilight hours, it's possible to shoot directly towards the light source without fear of overexposing the highlights. Under these circumstances, any objects will be rendered as a silhouette, so look for subjects with recognizable and pleasing outlines.

Experimenting with exposure at this time of day will impact the image in fairly drastic ways. A longer exposure will wash out colors near the horizon, but extend the blues into the sky, while reducing the exposure will intensify the colors that are nearest the light source.

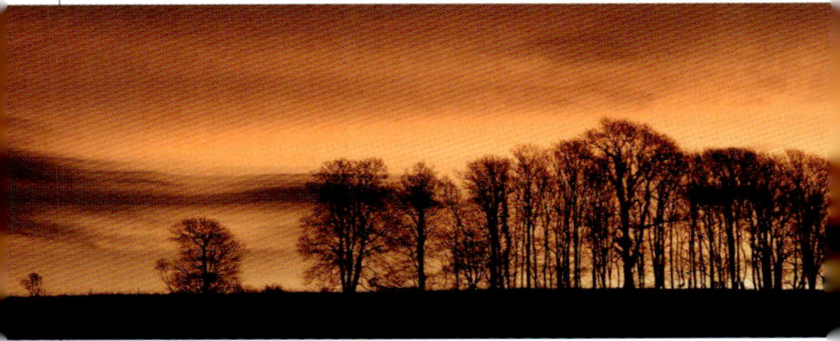

Clouds at twilight (above) can reflect dramatically a sun that's about to rise, or if unbroken destroy the subtle light altogether. A clear twilight sky (right) acts like a smooth reflective surface with the sun lying below the horizon.

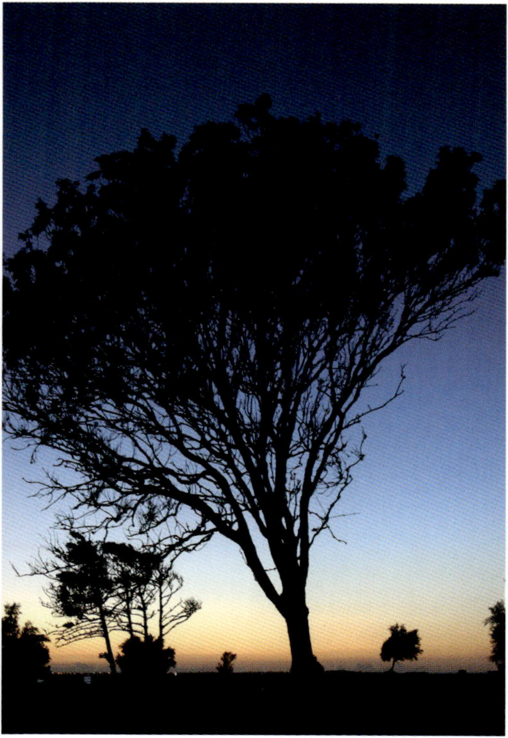

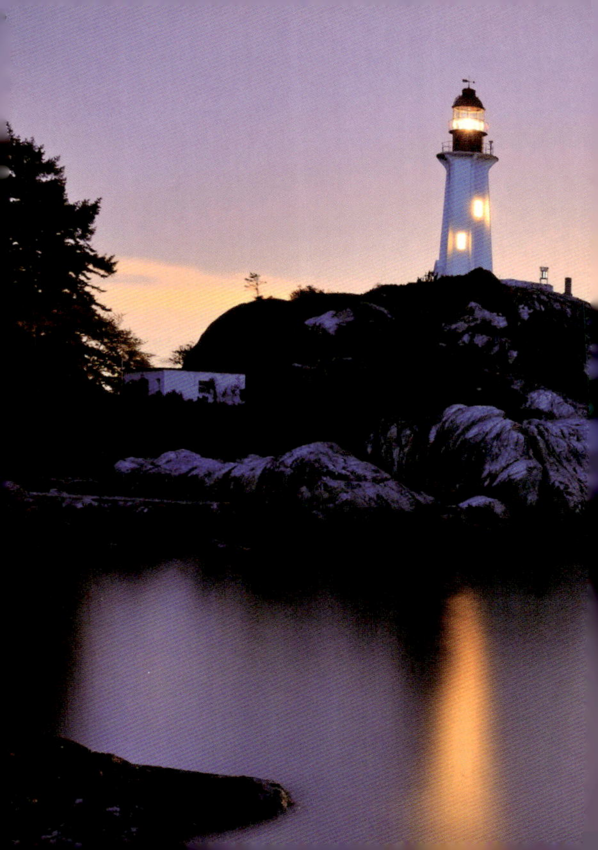

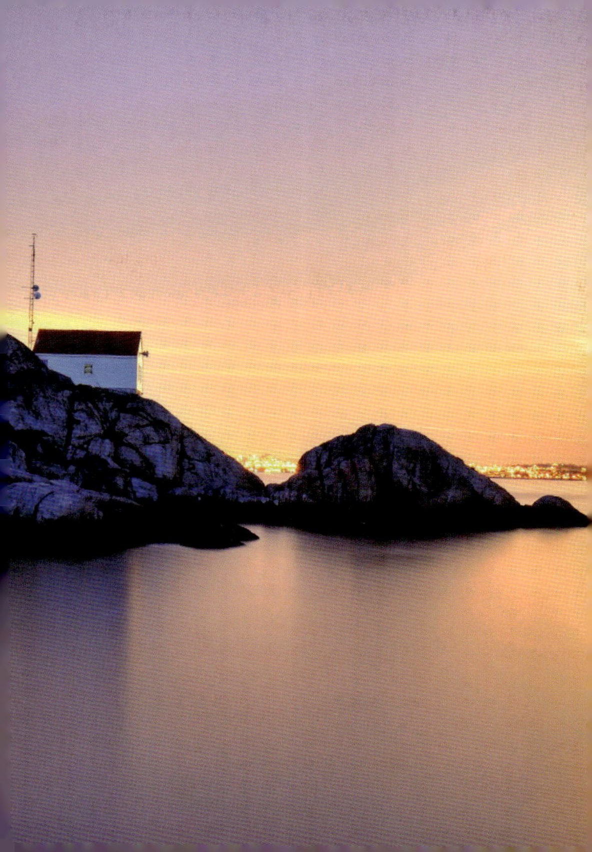

Sunrise and Sunset

There are few more evocative times of the day than the first hour following sunrise, or the last before sunset. However, the popularity of the so-called "Golden Hours" has arguably rendered them somewhat hackneyed. However, that doesn't mean to say you shouldn't bother attempting to capture a few of your own. As well as just relying on the richness of the colors, try to find another element that will add a certain resonance to the image.

Adjusting exposure will have the same effect as when shooting during twilight, however, with the sun above the horizon, shooting directly at it may result in a burned out, white ball. Try hiding the sun behind an object for more silhouette effects.

While sunsets are a source of rich, vibrant colors, your image will have greater impact if it forms the backdrop to a composition.

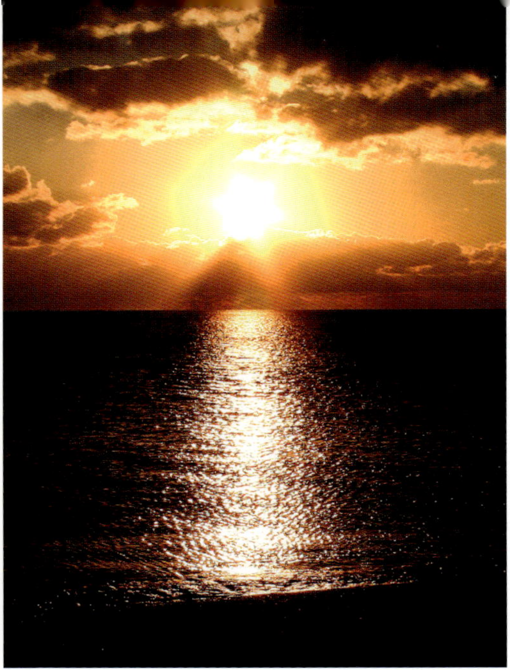

The reflective surface of water can help to reinforce a sunset, a fact recognized by many 19th century artists, such as Turner.

Morning and Afternoon

While perhaps less immediately striking than sunrise and sunset, morning and afternoon light has a great deal to recommend it. Shadows are still long, helping to emphasize form thanks to the modeling effect long shadows bring, and this modeling effect is often used in landscape images. The low, raking angle of the sun also helps to bring out the texture of objects, depending on their position in relation to that of the sun.

In terms of color, the higher sun provides a more neutral light, so if accurate colors are important, shoot when the sun is at least an hour or two away from the horizon.

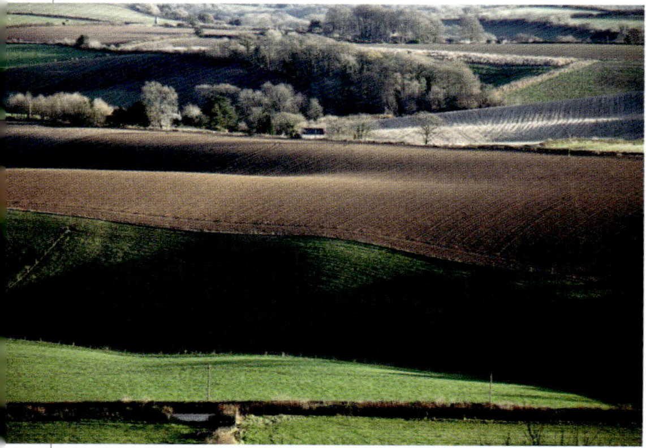

A clear winter afternoon in temperate Europe brings long shadows that can be successfully exploited for their modeling effect on rolling landscapes.

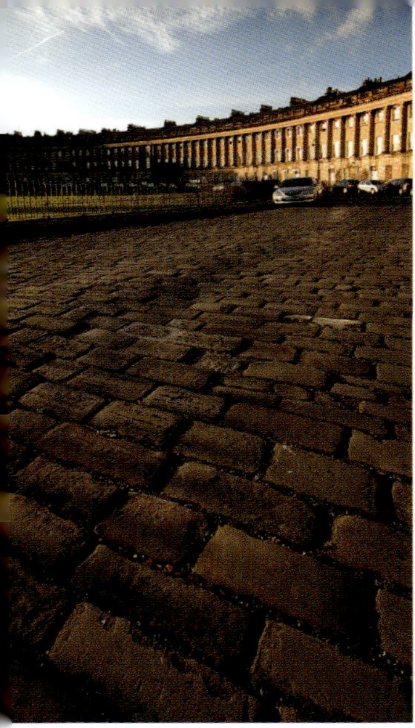

Side lighting, when the sun is to one side of the camera, reveals texture at its strongest.

Lighting effects

With the sun relatively low in the sky and casting long shadows, the morning and afternoon are ideal times to experiment with the camera at different angles relative to the sun; in front, behind, and to one side. This will provide different forms of lighting, each of which can have a dramatic effect on your subject, and which are covered on the following pages.

Side Lighting

With the sun to one side of the camera, and particularly in the morning or afternoon—exactly when depends on your latitude—when shadows are still long and somewhat unpredictable, you'll experience strong side lighting. Side lighting has a number of photographic benefits. First, it can help to outline the shape of an object, and so, as we've seen, create a modeling effect. Second, the pits and grooves, and peaks and troughs on an object's surface are most apparent with the long shadows that accompany side lighting. And finally, images under this type of lighting tend to exhibit strong contrast between light and shade.

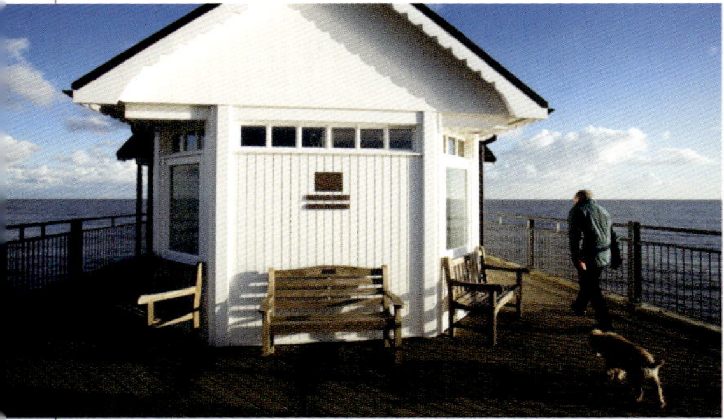

The long, raking shadows that you get with side lighting tend to create high-contrast images, with highlights juxtaposed with deep shadows. At the same time, the shadows help to reveal detail and texture. The individual boards that make up the front panel of this seaside hut would be much harder to distinguish if the hut had been lit from the front than from the side.

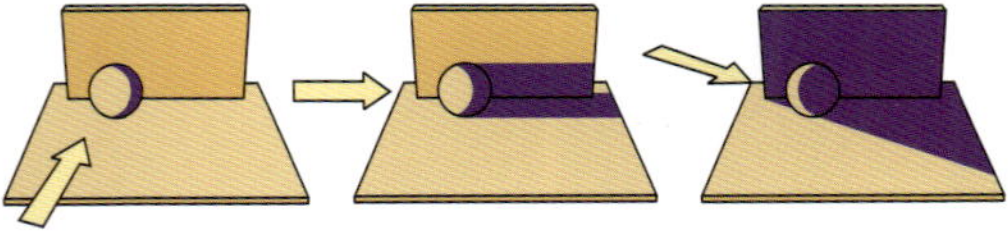

Light and shade

Side lighting produces the most distinct shadows. This sequence shows what happens as the direction of the sunlight moves from frontal to back. The shadows are smallest from the camera's viewpoint in frontal lighting, while in back lighting, shadows dominate to the extent that there are few sunlit parts to give local contrast. The maximum light/dark contrast is when the sun is at right angles to the camera.

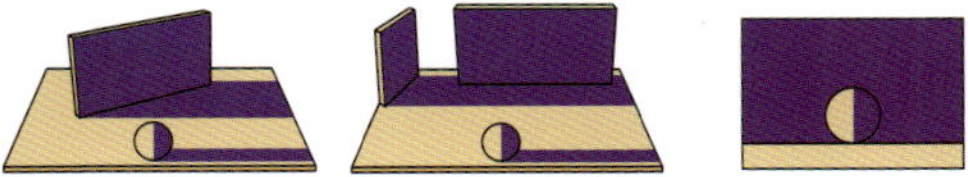

High contrast

High contrast is typical of many side-lit scenes. The lighting is at right angles to the view, and thus the shadows are too. As the diagrams show, a surface needs to be angled only slightly away from the sun, or be shaded by quite a narrow obstruction, to give a high light/dark contrast.

Shooting at right angles to the sun can add a linear, horizontal component to the image.

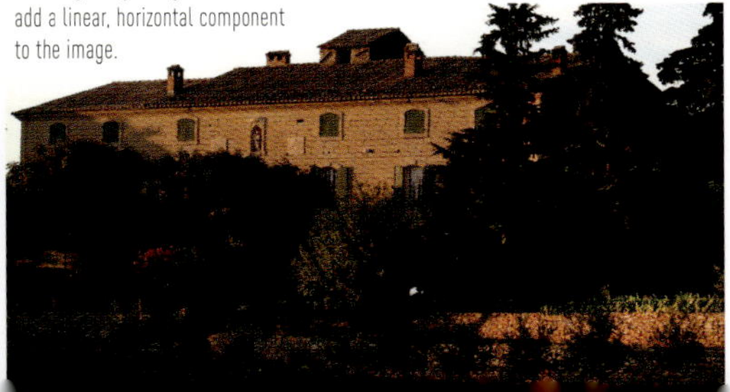

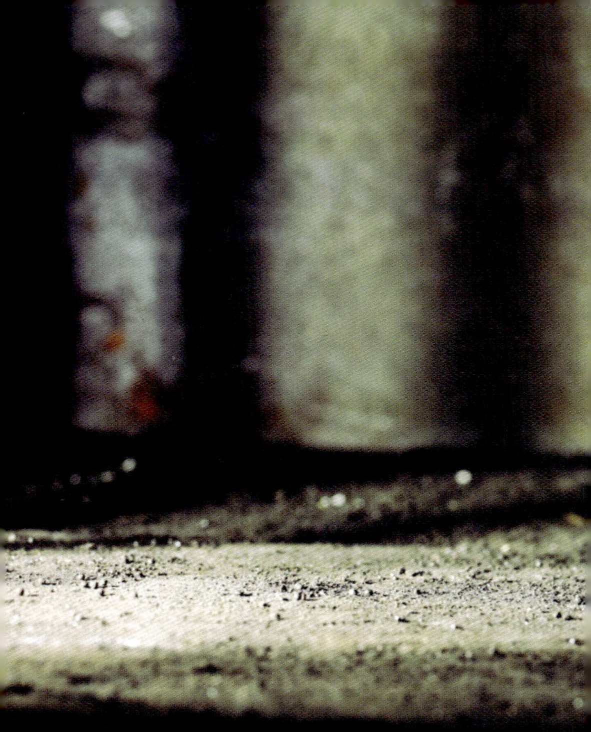

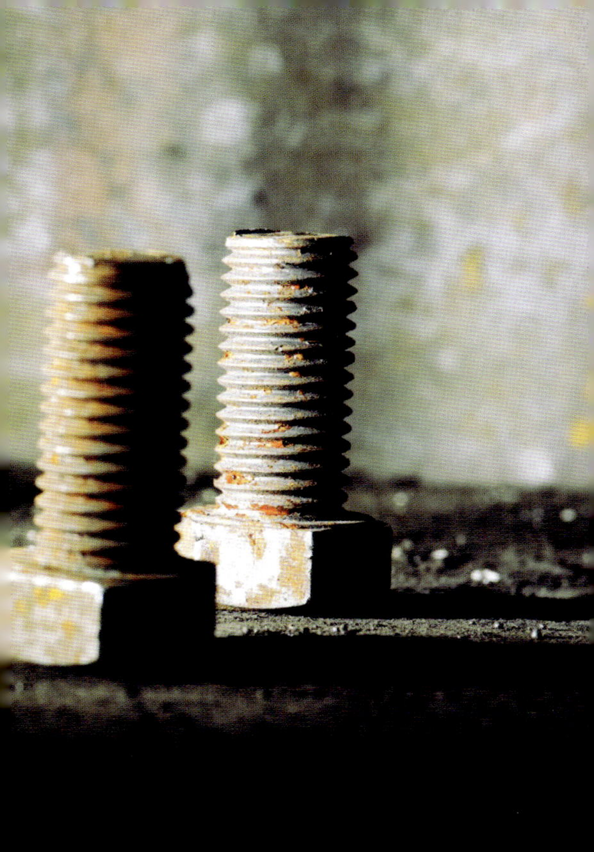

Frontal Lighting

Frontal lighting is when the sun is behind you, so that the light strikes the subject full-on. Unlike side lighting, frontal lighting can be free of shadows, as often the sun's rays run along the exact same axis as the camera's viewpoint, so any shadows are cast are often behind the subject, hidden from view.

For this reason, frontal lighting can create a rather flat, two-dimensional feel to your images—there's little in the way of modeling effect here. Instead, look for saturated colors which will reproduce well in frontal lighting, and interesting outlines that stand out against a plain background.

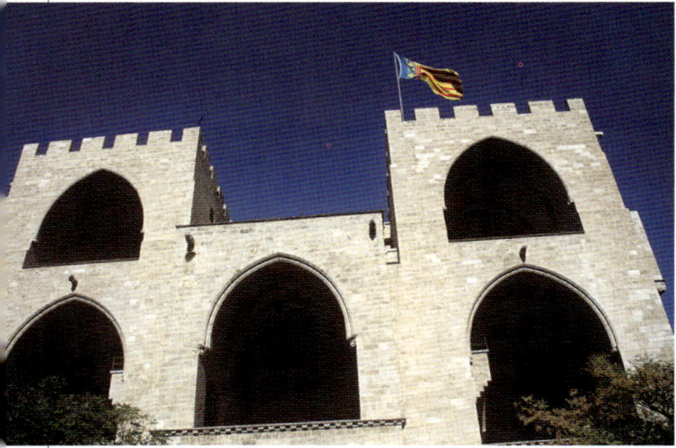

Frontal lighting will create the deepest colored skies in your picture, as in this shot of an ancient gatehouse in Spain.

However, the head-on lighting makes the structure look rather two-dimensional.

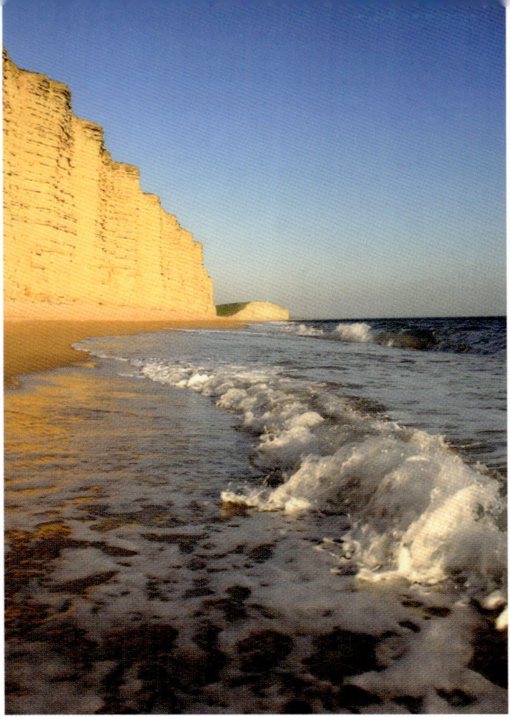

Frontally lit scenes often rely on strong color contrast and well-defined form to make the image successful.

Back Lighting

Shooting directly into the sun produces back lighting. The resulting images are usually high-contrast, with perhaps the best-known example being the silhouette (see pages 78–79). But that's not the whole story with back lighting. With the sun out of the field of view, however, and particularly if it's not very bright, such as late in the day or early in the morning, it's possible to keep some detail in the subject. This can create more interesting and subtle back-lit images.

A light evening haze combined with back lighting creates a strong aerial perspective of receding hills in near silhouette. The time of day and the fact that the sun is out of the frame has helped retain some detail in the foreground and middle distance.

The normal rules for backlighting do not apply with translucent subjects. The light shines through the petals of these tulips, intensifying their colors against the carefully chosen, dark background.

Types of back lighting

There are four basic kinds of effect when shooting towards the sun. Shooting directly into the sun produces a hard silhouette against a concentrated area of brightness. A higher angle into a reflective surface, such as water, also gives a silhouette, but the bright background will be larger. When the sun is higher and out of the frame, some shadow detail will be visible. With edge lighting, the background is dark enough to show the brightly lit edge of the subject.

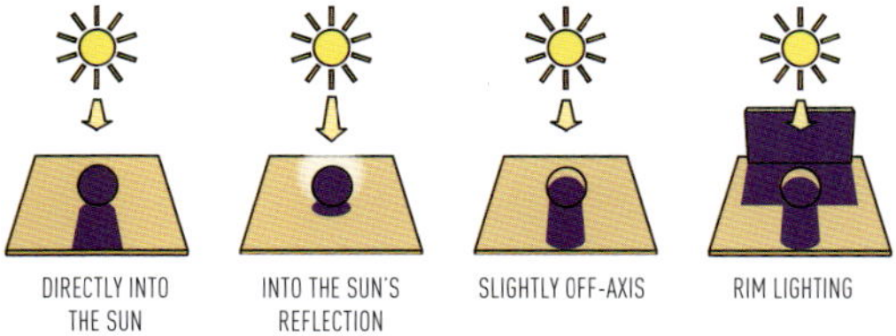

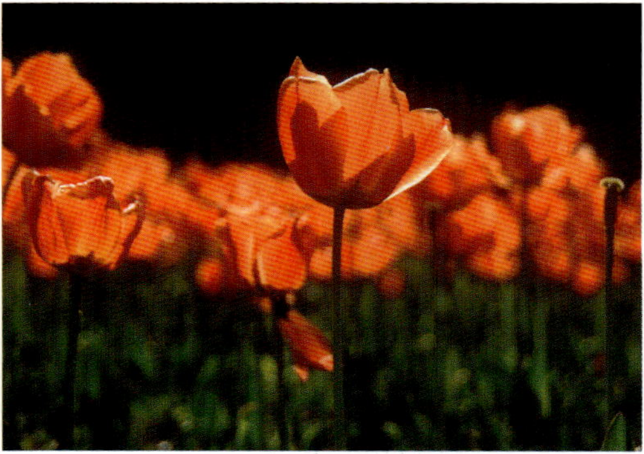

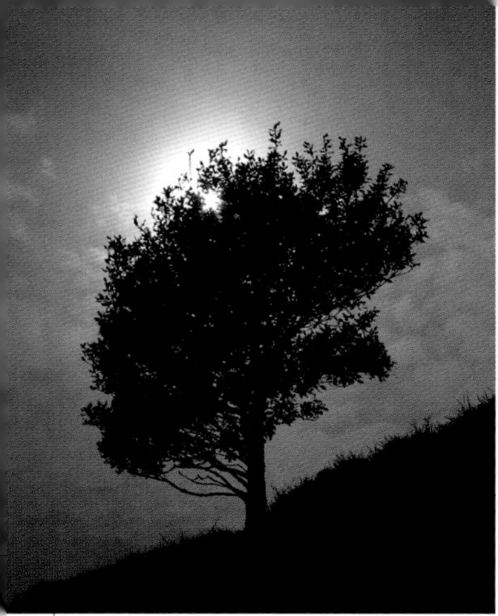

Objects that possess an interesting and easily recognizable shape are usually the best subjects for silhouettes. Shooting against a clear, uncluttered sky will show the subject off at its best.

Silhouette

Silhouettes are most successful when the subject of the photo has an interesting and obvious outline. In a clear sky with a high, bright sun, it's usually necessary to place the object directly between the camera and the sun to record any outline shape at all, and this can occasionally restrict your choice of subject.

In terms of exposure, as silhouettes show little, if any detail, you can experiment quite freely with exposure settings and still end up with an acceptable result. However, be wary of lens flare when shooting directly into the sun. This can either manifest itself as rows of increasingly sized abnormally colored patches, or more subtly, simply washed out or faded regions.

The sun's reflection

Any surface texture tends to diffuse the reflection and spread the bright area. The angle of reflection is critical. Either move higher or lower, or wait for the sun's position to change.

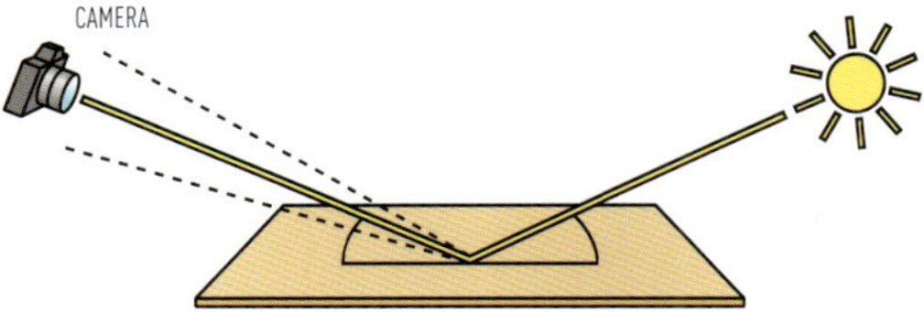

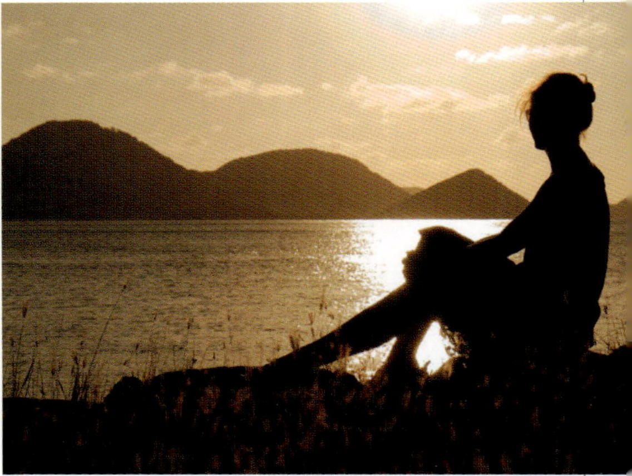

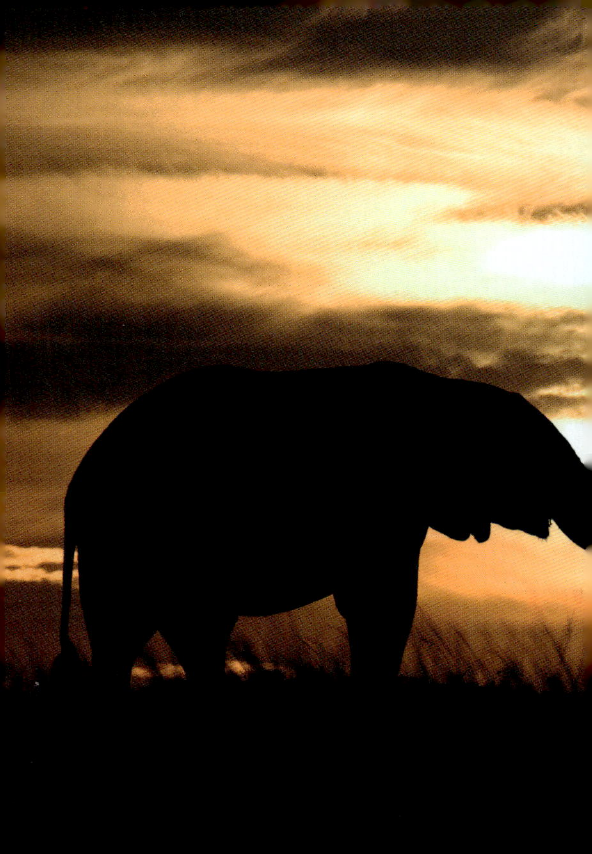

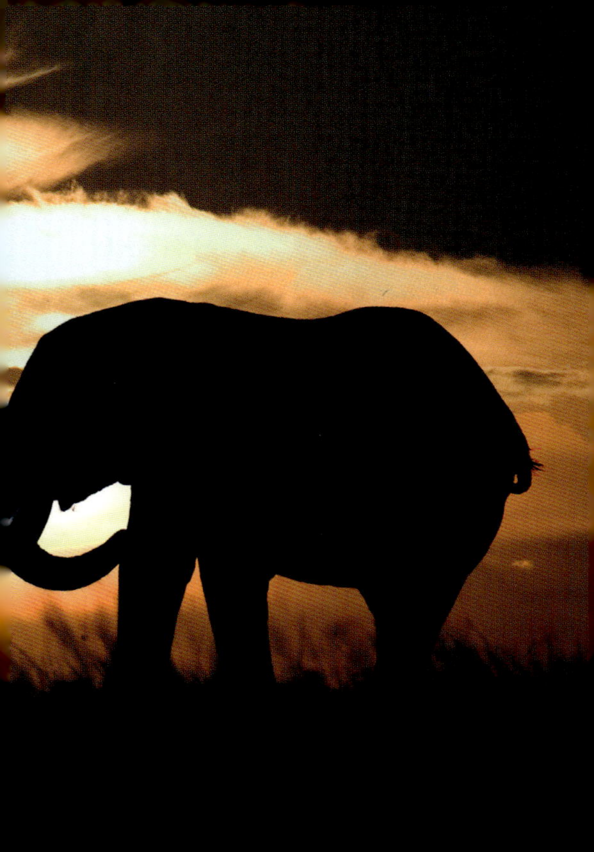

Edge Lighting

When the light strikes the object from behind, but off to one side, a phenomenon known as edge, or rim lighting may become apparent. This can be highly atmospheric as the edges of objects are imbued with a soft, glowing effect. The glow is actually a form of lens flare, and to that extent you need to be able to control the severity of the effect, making sure that the edge lighting is desirable and not actually detracting from the image.

The amount of glow is governed by the physical attributes of the object you're photographing—a hard surface will result in a very thin, consistent glowing edge, while a softer, more fibrous surface will produce a much larger and less predictable flare.

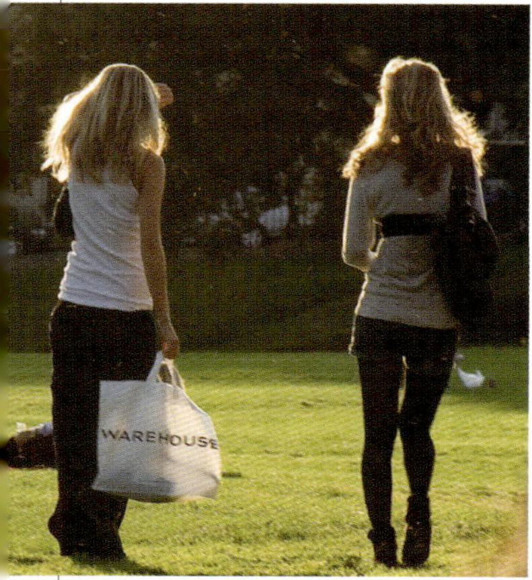

Shot in late afternoon, with the sun low in the sky, this image shows the effect of back lighting when the sun is not directly in front of the subject. Compare the extent of the glow present in the hair with the glow around the clothes.

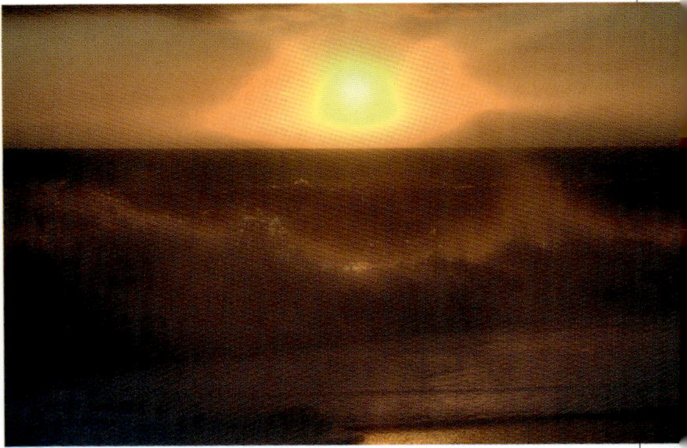

Reducing the risk of flare

- Fit a customized lens shade made by the camera manufacturer for your particular lens.
- Keep the lens clean. A film of grease or dust makes flare much worse. Regularly check the lens and wipe it with a lens cloth.
- Remove any filters. Filters, however good, add another layer of glass that increases the risk of flare. Try removing any that might be fitted.
- Use a properly coated lens. High-quality, multi-coated lenses are less prone to flare than cheaper ones. Use the best lenses you can afford. Unlike camera models, quality lenses will hold their value.
- If you don't have a lens shade, use your hand or a piece of card as far forward as you can reach, just out of frame, to cast a shadow over the lens.

Lens flare creates the warm glow that suffuses this telephoto view of breaking waves. Whether you see this as a problem of weakened contrast or as a pictorial addition is largely a matter of taste.

High Sun

At around noon, when the sun is high in a cloudless sky, light is at its most neutral color, and shadows are generally short. There are no natural warm tones or raking shadows along the ground to add atmosphere or drama at this time of day, and for many photographers it's an unappealing time to shoot. The lack of shadows in open country can result in flat-looking landscapes, while shots of people will result in shaded eyes and unattractive shadows running down the face.

However, the consistent and neutral light will result in accurately colored and crisp images containing clear and bright detail. Subjects, therefore, with interesting form and color, such as some architecture for example, will come out well in this light.

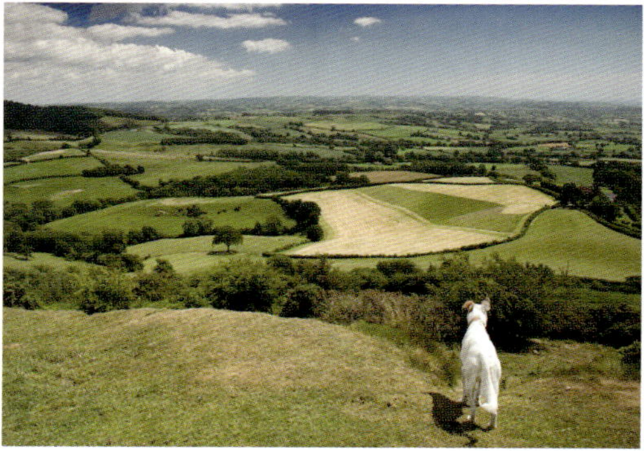

Despite the lack of any modeling shadows, this landscape is successful for its clarity of detail, far reaching view and honest colors.

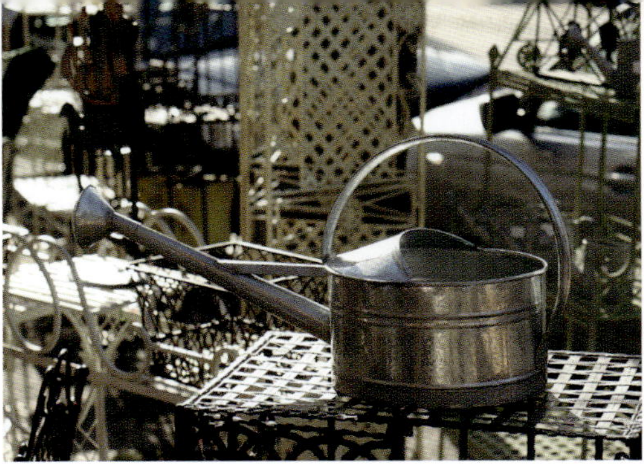

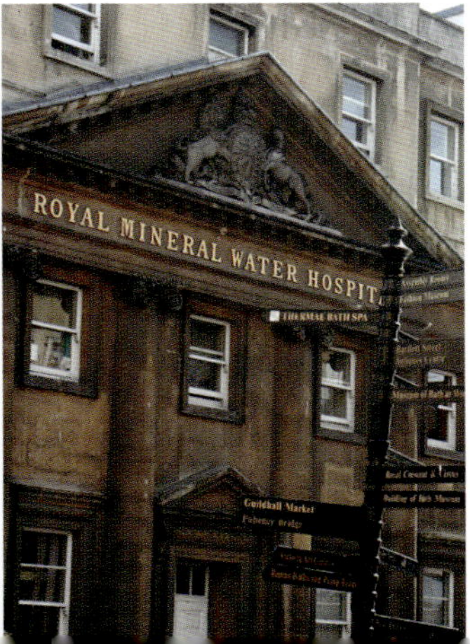

A high, uninterrupted sun creates a crisp, bright, and neutral light that shows off detail to its best advantage.

A potentially difficult and confusing image to "read" is made simpler thanks to there being no shadows to break up the architectural lines or to partly obscure the signage.

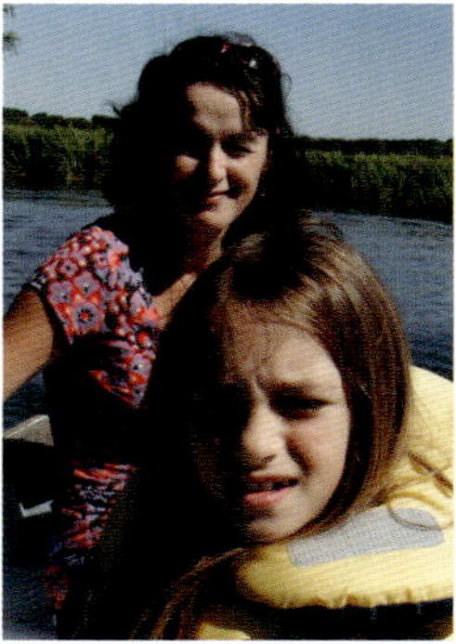

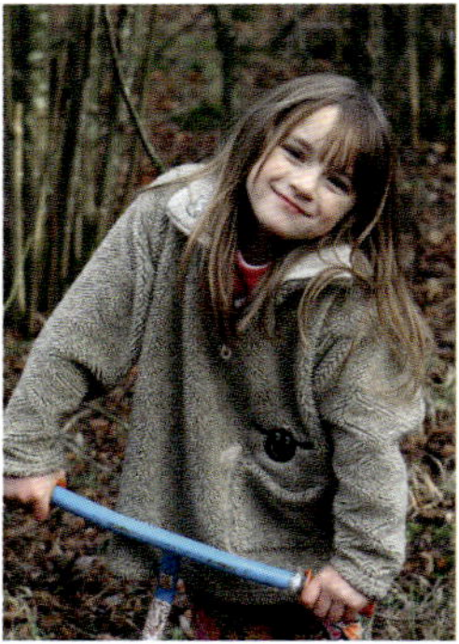

Harsh light (left) rarely works well with portraits—the strong shadows are unflattering. Soft lighting (right) is far kinder to the subject.

Soft and Hard Light

The quality of lighting is not just dependent on its angle and color; it also depends on how diffuse the light is. The more that the light is scattered, the softer and less direct it becomes, and shadows appear within the picture less distinctly.

Outdoors, it is cloud that has the greatest effect on the harshness of the sunlight. Direct light from the sun that has not passed through clouds is "harsh" or "hard," and creates well-defined shadows. But when the light passes through clouds, the water vapor diffracts the light in a multitude of directions, creating a softer, more even illumination. Light can also be softened by dust particles, as on a hazy day, or by reflections from the ground, buildings, and other surfaces.

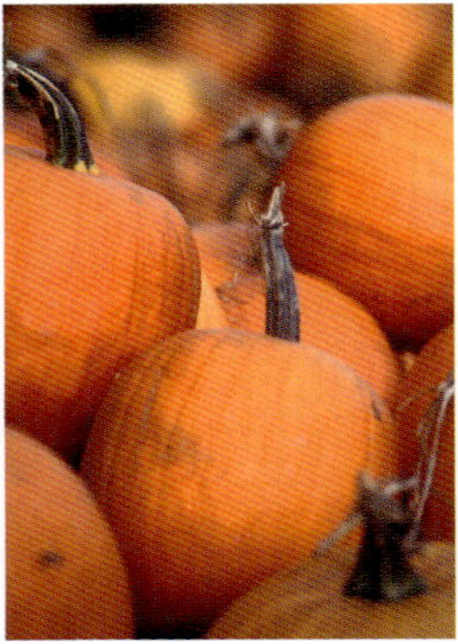

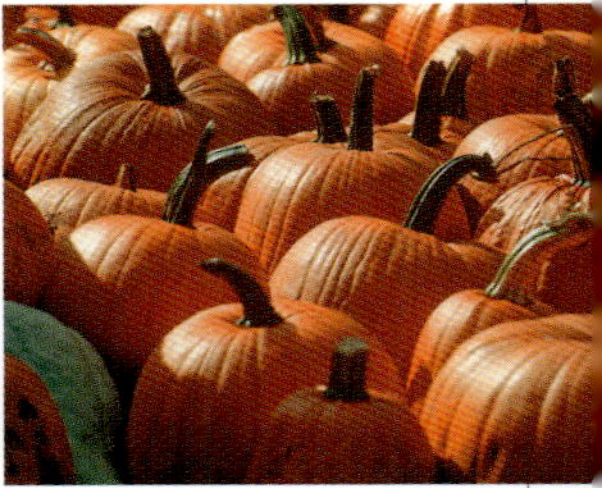

The strong shadows created by direct sunlight are helpful in this composition (right), as the shading accentuates the form of the pumpkins. Soft lighting (left) creates a much more subdued picture, with softer colors.

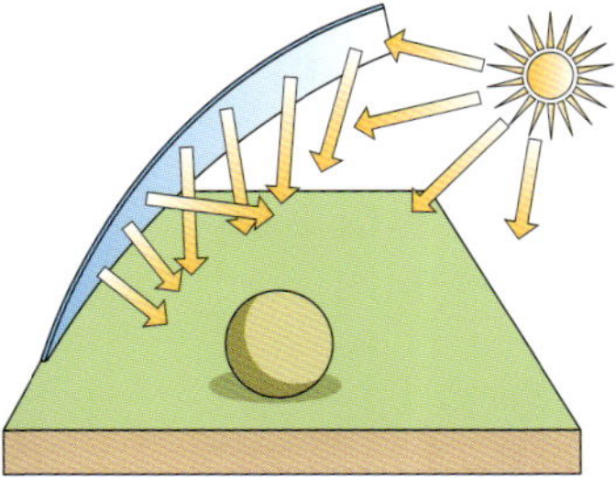

On a sunny day, light rays have only the atmosphere to pass through, so cast strong shadows. Clouds, however, acts as giant diffusers, providing light from all angles.

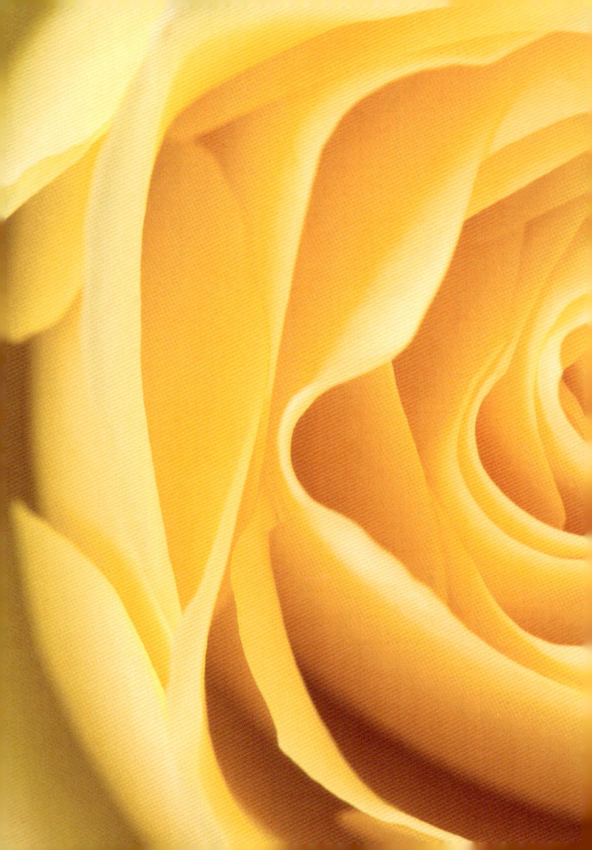

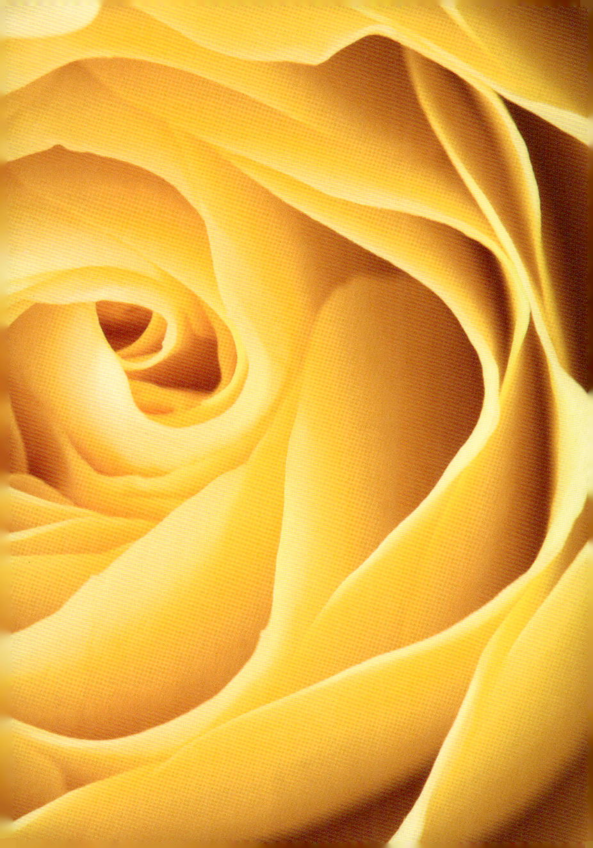

Haze

Haze is an atmospheric phenomenon created by the scattering of light due to the presence of fine dust, moisture, and occasionally pollution in the air. Its effect is to soften light and reduce color and contrast. The impact haze will have on an image increases with distance, and for this reason haze can bring an added sense of depth and perspective.

In certain circumstances, with very fine particles in the atmosphere, shorter wavelengths of light (ultraviolet) are scattered more than longer wavelengths of light, creating a blue, hazy effect.

Depending on your subject and composition, haze can either add to the strength of the composition or render it simply vague and washed out.

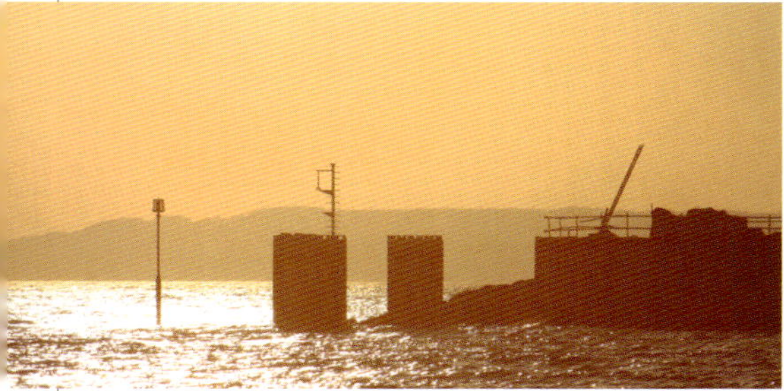

Hazy conditions are often most noticeable late in the day or early in the morning, when the light rays have more atmosphere to travel through. Here the hazy conditions help to delineate between the middle distance and far distance objects, creating a sense of depth.

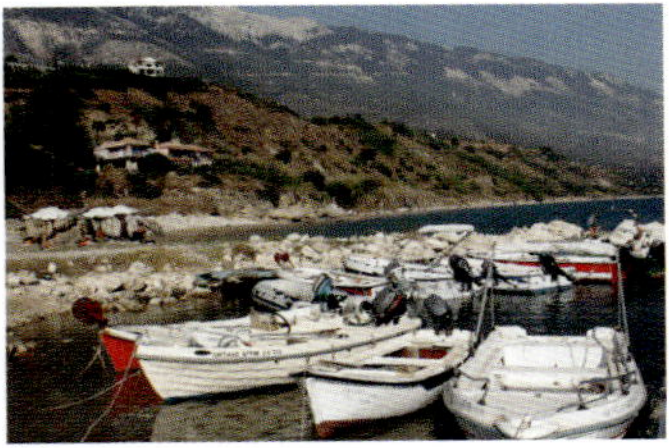

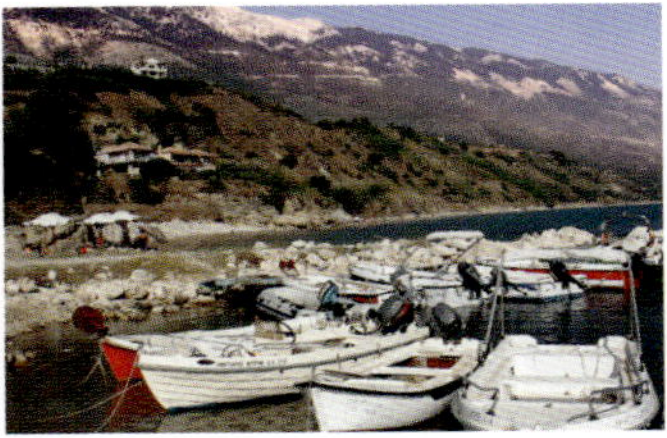

The distant hills in this shot have a distinctly blue tinge to them (top). Attaching a UV filter to the front of the lens brings back some of the real color (below).

Ways of reducing haze

Haze can be unwelcome if it hides detail, color, and crispness. The following are ways of reducing it:

Ultraviolet filter This works on the short wavelengths only, so the effect is unlikely to be total.

Polarizing filter This works most strongly at right angles to the sun (in side lighting) and gives an overall improvement.

Frontal or side lighting Either of these is preferable to back lighting, which exaggerates the effect of haze.

Avoid distant views The closer you shoot, the less atmosphere, and the less haze. For this reason, a wide-angle shot that captures objects nearer to the camera, will be less affected by haze than a telephoto shot.

Low-light Scenes

A wide variety of scenes can produce powerfully atmospheric images when shot in low-light—from the bright, mixed lighting of a cityscape to the subdued, haunting light of a late evening rural scene.

Getting the right exposure is critical in low-light situations. If you overexposethe image you'll lose the atmosphere as the light you're trying to capture will become washed out. However, underexpose the image and so much detail will be lost that it will be difficult to discern the composition.

This photograph was taken in an early winter's evening. Remnants of the day are visible as a band of pale orange, but the lack of light has removed the color from everything else in the image, creating a very soft and subdued composition.

Low-light and noise

Noise is always going to be a concern in low-light or night conditions, as it is most easily detected in dark or shadow regions, of which there will be many in shots taken at this time. Always shoot with the lowest possible ISO setting, which will inevitably require a long exposure. To avoid camera-shake always use a tripod, or a sturdy surface on which to rest the camera. Most digital SLRs have a noise-reduction facility, so experiment with the setting to see what impact it has on your low-light images.

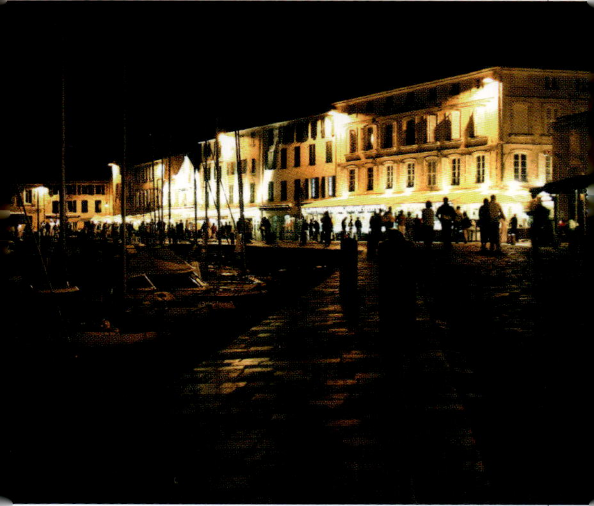

It's not just large metropolises that make good urban subjects for night-time shots. Smaller towns will usually have enough interesting lighting to create good atmospheric images.

Moonlight

Our perception of moonlight is a dim, eerie light that reveals little color. Ironically, your initial photographs captured by moonlight may actually look as if they have been photographed during the day. This is because the camera's meter will automatically set a sufficiently long exposure until the amount of light captured by the sensor compares with the amount normally captured during the day. To "correct" this, you need to reduce the metered exposure by a stop or two, either by shooting manually or using exposure compensation. You may also find that your images appear more colorful than you anticipated. This is because, although our eyes are poor at perceiving color under moonlit conditions, the camera's sensor is not. To replicate your perception, either reduce color saturation in camera, or later during post-production.

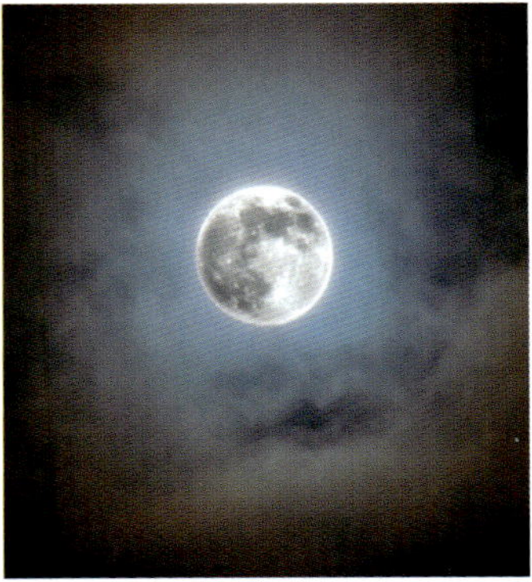

Photographing the moon itself requires a long telephoto lens if you want the moon to fill a good portion of the frame. Although the brightness of the moon may allow for shutter speeds of around 1/250 sec, you'll still need to use a tripod to avoid camera-shake.

Photographing the moon

For the moon to be a reasonable size in the frame, a powerful telephoto is needed, 400mm is the minimum. With such lenses, the maximum aperture of the lens is likely to be quite small, unless you have an exceptionally expensive example, so exposure control and bracketing is usually done by altering the shutter speed. The limit to the slowest shutter speed is the movement of the moon's image in the frame. As the moon's image moves at a rate of its own diameter every two minutes, an exposure of one second or longer, with a 400mm lens, will cause blurring.

With the moon being the only relatively bright object in the frame, exposing to at least capture the shape and basic form of other objects will result in the moon overexposing. Not such an issue when the moon is only a small element of the composition, but more problematic if the moon were to play a larger role.

Lightning

Photographs of lightning can make for extremely dramatic images. The main difficulty with photographing lightning is predicting where it's going to strike and when. Fortunately, lightning tends to be fairly localized, so if you spot a lightning flash in one part of the sky, there's a good chance that any further flashes are likely to occur in the same region.

In terms of exposure, capturing lightning during the day is extremely challenging. Using a tripod and remote shutter release, expose for the ambient light, and then compensate by reducing exposure by one or two stops, depending on how close you think you'll be to the strike. It's then really a question of anticipating the strike and having quick reactions, pressing the shutter release as soon as you see the flash.

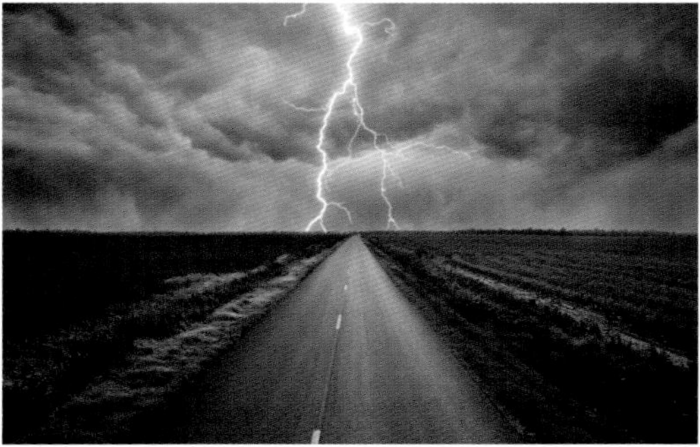

Photographing lightning during the day is all about anticipating where the next strike will occur, and having sufficiently fast reactions to capture it.

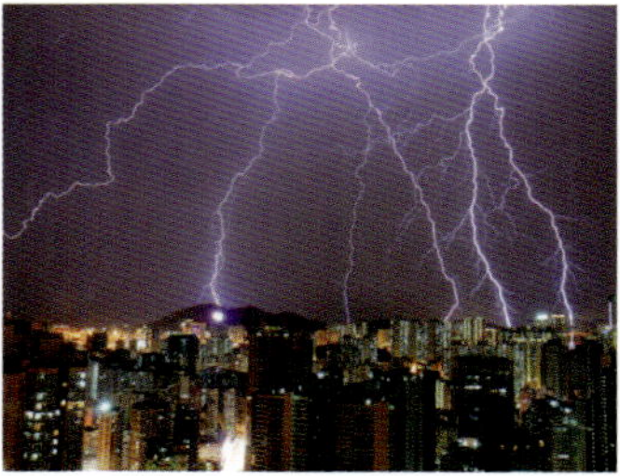

At night you can use the bulb setting to capture lightning, as the lack of ambient light will not lead to overexposed shots.

The best time to photograph lightning is at dusk or at night, remembering to turn your flash off. At these times, the ambient lighting is low enough for you to use a bulb exposure, keeping the shutter open continuously until after the flash. You'll still need to avoid keeping the shutter open for too long to avoid overexposing, particularly if there's still some light in the sky. That requires a certain amount of anticipation and appreciation of the length of time between each flash.

In terms of aperture, there are no exact settings. The table below provides some guidelines.

Lightning brightness	ISO	Aperture
Very close (< 100 meters/yards)	100	f/16–f/22
Relatively close (up to 1 km/0.5 miles)	100	f/11
Distant lightning (5–10 km/3–6 miles)	100	f/5.6
Far lightning (10–20 km/6–12 miles)	200	f/4–f/5.6
Remote lightning (20-50 km/12–30 miles)	200	f/2.8

Fireworks

Much of the rules for photographing lightning can be applied to photographing fireworks, even though fireworks are much easier to predict.

Stake out the best place from which to photograph. Clearly you need an interrupted view, but it's also worth considering which way any breeze is blowing. If you can, position yourself so the breeze is blowing either to one side of you or onto your back. Fireworks can be very smokey, and you don't want your images marred by palls of smoke.

Again, set the camera on a tripod and use a remote shutter release. Manually focus on the area where the fireworks are going to light the sky, and use a focal length setting that captures most of that area of sky. Use a fairly small aperture of around f/8 or f/16, which will help to keep the fireworks in focus, and wait for the show to start.

Using bulb exposure, watch the firework trails as they shoot into the sky. Open the shutter before the firework actually explodes and keep it open for as long as the firework lights the sky. They usually come in batches, making it easier to anticipate the next series.

As with lightning, make sure the flash is disabled, and remember that although you'll be shooting in the dark, fireworks are very bright, so keeping the shutter open for too long to capture multiple bursts may end up with an overexposed result. If you want, experiment by holding a black card in front of the lens between each burst and taking it away for the next burst.

As you gain experience, try capturing multiple bursts by placing a black card or piece of black foam in front of the lens, to cover it between each explosion.

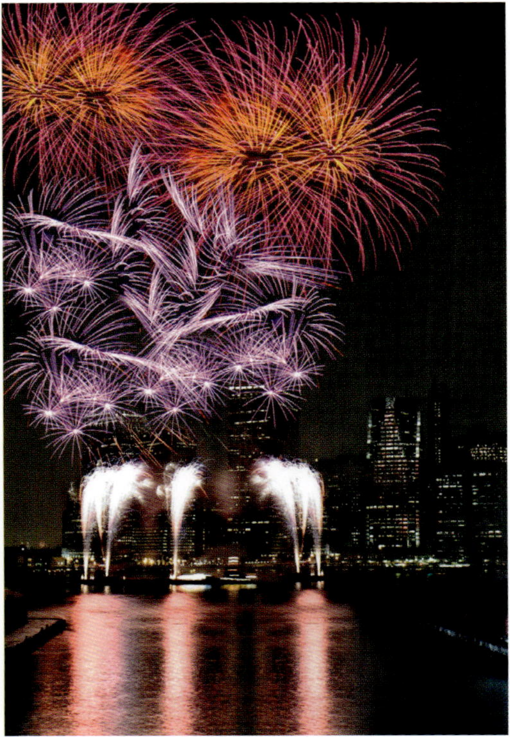

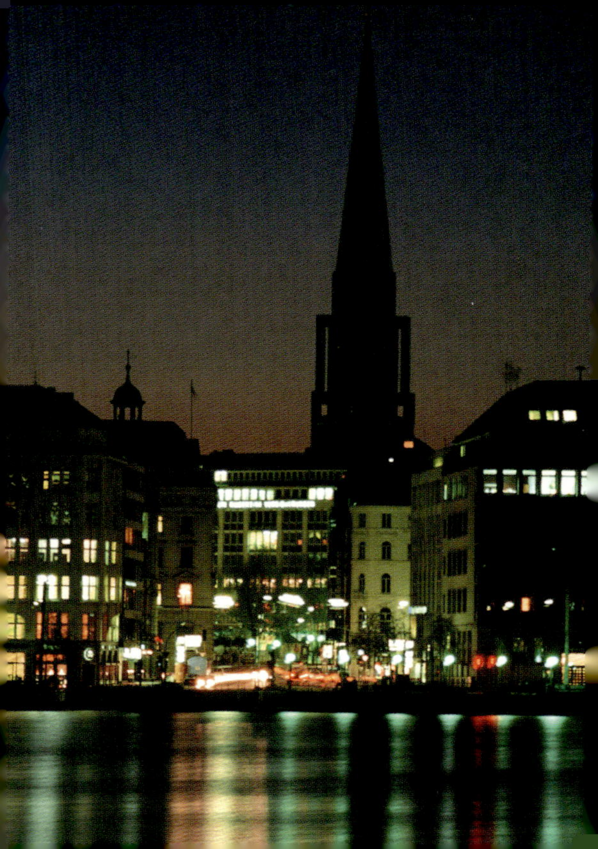

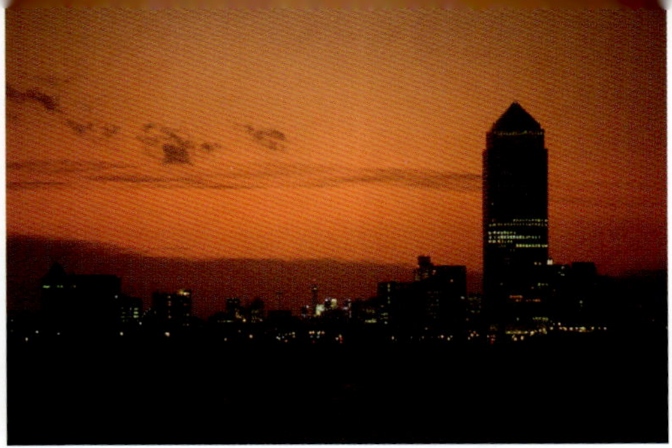

Water always adds atmosphere to any night city scene.

Get to your location early, before the sun has fully set.

City Lights

Night-time city scenes can make for spectacular images, whether it's the illuminated buildings of a commercial district, or the brightly colored display lights of a downtown entertainment area.

Choosing when to photograph such sights is the key to capturing successful night shots. In many cases, the best time to photograph is actually before night has set in—in other words at dusk when there is still some remnant of the day left in the sky. The ambient lighting helps balance the exposure with the bright display lights, and generally makes getting the right exposure much easier than photographing when the sky is pitch black.

Finding the right location from which to shoot is also key, so plan ahead during the day and get to your location in plenty of time. Exposure times will vary, but you'll certainly need a tripod and a remote shutter release. Start with an aperture setting of around f/8, and keep reviewing your shots to check your results.

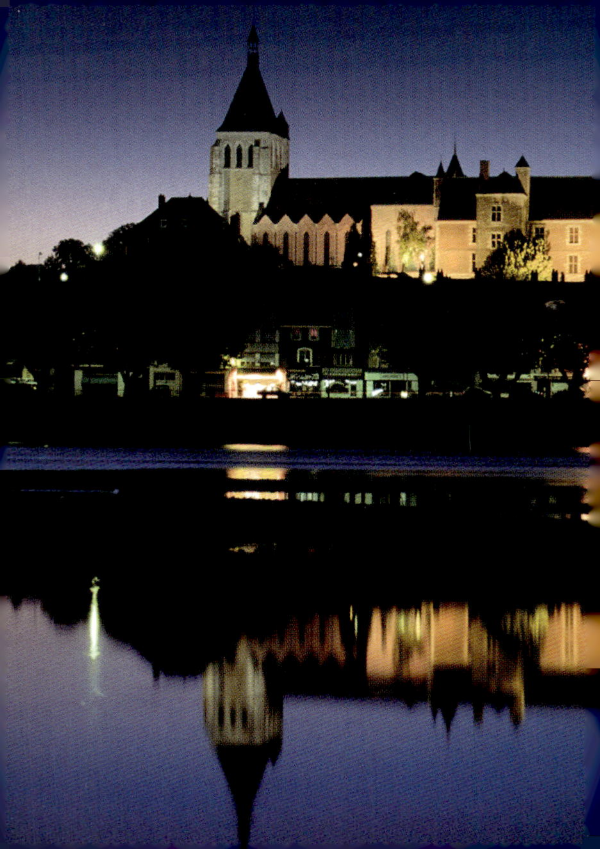

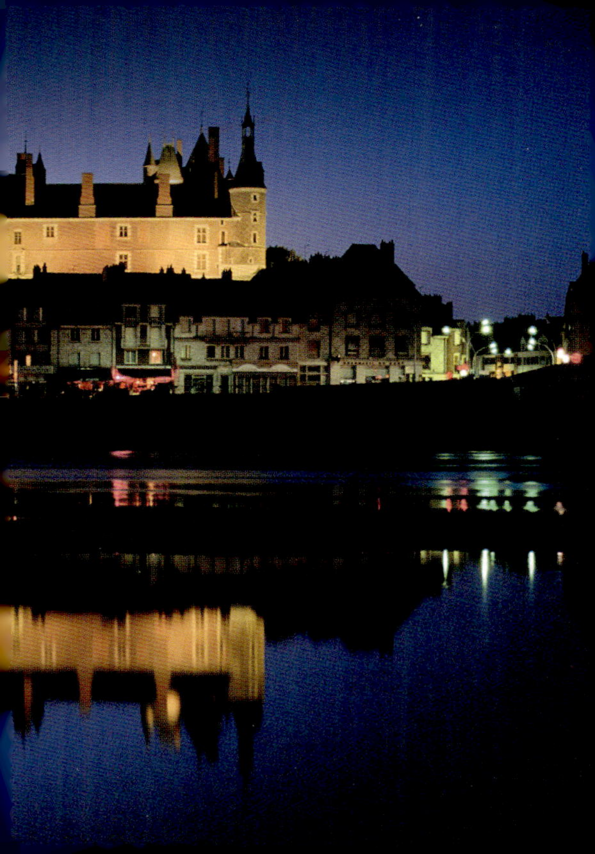

High Key

Shots that comprise mostly white or light tones, with few middle and/or dark tones, are called "high key." Unless you work in a studio, where you have total control over the lighting, shooting a high-key image depends somewhat on being in the right place at the right time. High-key landscapes, for example, need to exhibit generally low contrast, so pale, hazy, or light gray skies are the order, combined with a pale or light-toned setting—a blanket of snow or a light, sandy beach, for example, provide the ideal settings for a high-key image.

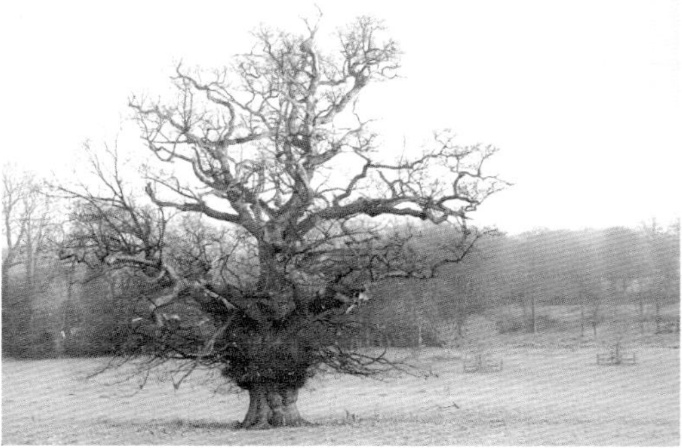

High-key images are generally, but not exclusively, exhibited as black and white pictures. You can either use the black and white setting on your camera, or shoot Raw and convert to black and white during post-production. The latter method makes sure you also have a color version.

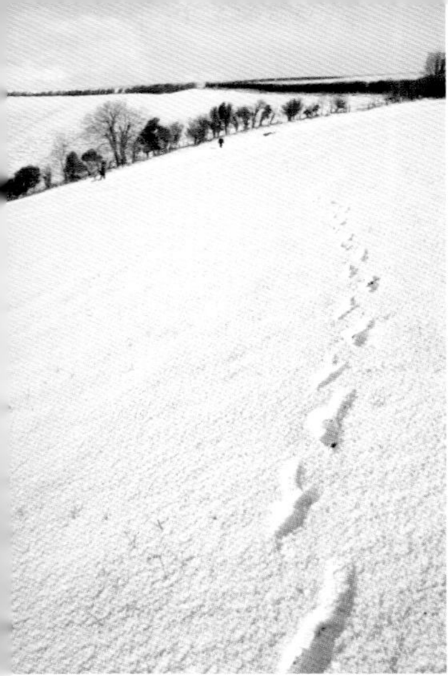

A recent heavy snow fall creates an expanse of white, combined with a pale blue winter sky—the ideal ingredients for this high-key shot. The only dark tones are made up from the leading line of footprints which bring the viewer into the scene, and the diagonal line of trees and hedgerow beyond, which add depth to the image.

This portrait exhibits the two main qualities of a high-key image—light and delicate. With high-key images you don't need to worry if areas overexpose as here. This is the result of increasing exposure compensation at the time of shooting by +2. The image was further lightened using image-editing software.

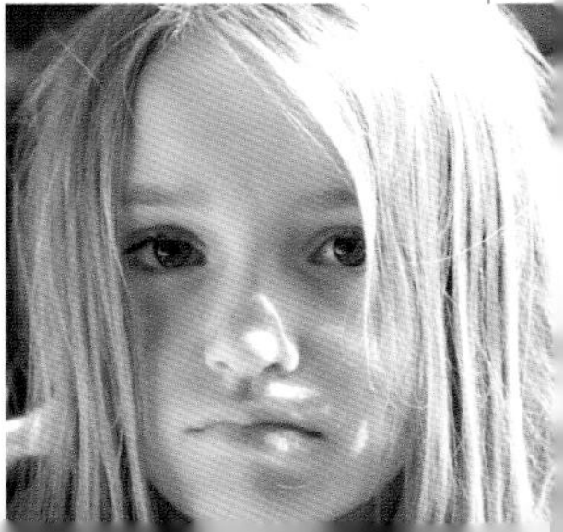

Low Key

In the way that high-key images rely on a preponderance of light tones to create their delicate and airy atmosphere, so low-key images rely on mainly dark tones to create a brooding and dramatic atmosphere.

Stormy weather conditions provide the ideal backdrop to low-key landscapes, with masses of threatening cloud and dimly lit subjects. Underexposure can help to emphasize the dark, brooding nature of low-key images, and just as blown highlights are not an issue with high-key photographs, don't worry if large shadow areas of your low-key image fill in to pure black.

Urban and landscape scenes are ideal low-key subjects, and while the light tones of high key make for delicate portraits of children, low key can be used successfully for more brooding portraits.

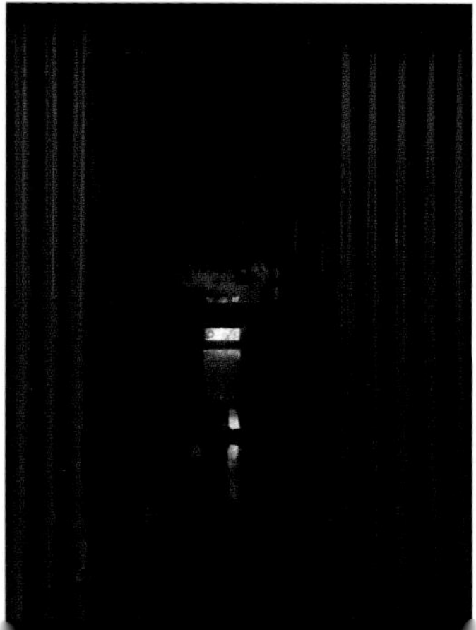

A low-key treatment adds a sense of mystery to this shot taken through the window of a Methodist chapel, with the window opposite offering the only relief from the otherwise somber atmosphere.

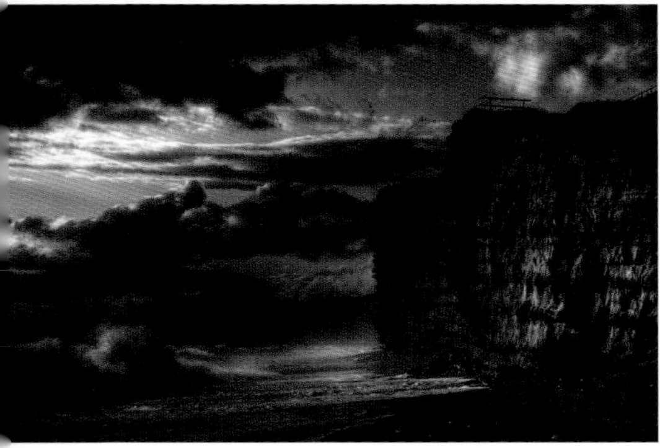

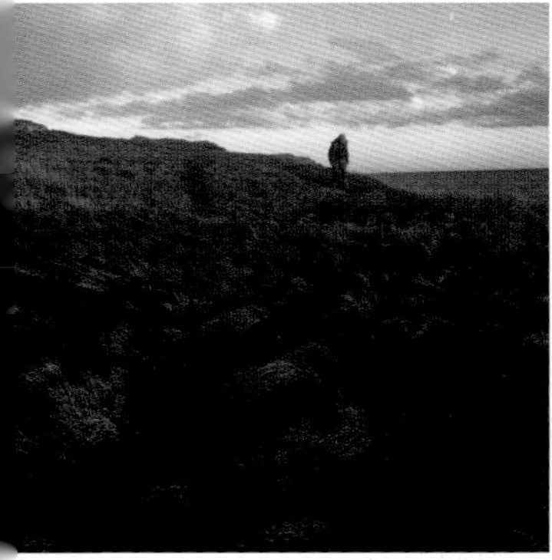

A classic low-key image, featuring threatening clouds and stormy seas. Exposure compensation was set to −2.

Exposure for this low-key shot was kept to a point where the grass was still visible, as its texture added to the impact of the image.

Expose for the Highlights

Even today's sophisticated digital SLRs can sometimes struggle when attempting to capture a scene containing very bright highlights and dark shadows. When the natural dynamic range of the scene exceeds that of the camera, it's simply not possible to record detail in both highlights and shadows.

When this happens you have various options. First, if it's the sky that's causing the problem, you can fix a neutral graduated filter to the front of the lens to help balance the highlights and shadows. Alternatively, you could take two or more shots of the same scene, exposing in turn for the highlights and shadows, and combine them on a computer to make a High Dynamic Range (HDR) image (see page 53). If neither of those options is possible, then the safest option is to expose for the highlights. Take a light reading from the brightest element of the composition (ideally using the spot or partial metering pattern), use exposure lock to

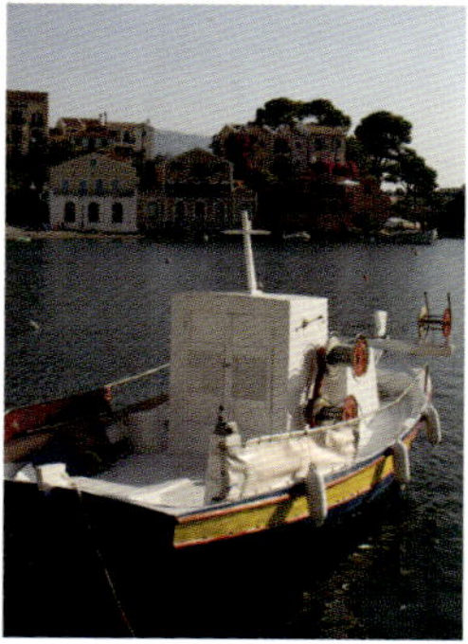

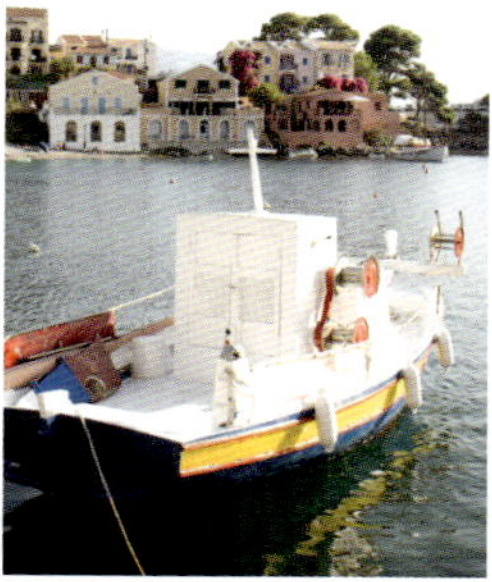

retain the exposure reading, recompose the shot, and fire the shutter. Check the results on the camera's LCD screen, using the histogram, the image replay, and highlight alert functions. Ideally, you'll have recorded detail in the brightest parts of the scene, leaving the darkest areas (hopefully not too many) pure black.

Although filled-in shadow areas are not ideal, they are visually far less distracting than areas of detail-free white. Furthermore, particularly if you have shot using the Raw format, you may find that you can retrieve a fair amount of detail from the shadow regions during post-production, whereas blown highlights are rarely recoverable.

Of course, there are exceptions to this rule, notably if the highlight areas are small in relation to the shadows, or if the highlight detail is not necessary to convey the image (such as specular highlights). Generally though, when the contrast of a scene is too high for your camera to retain all the information, expose for the highlights.

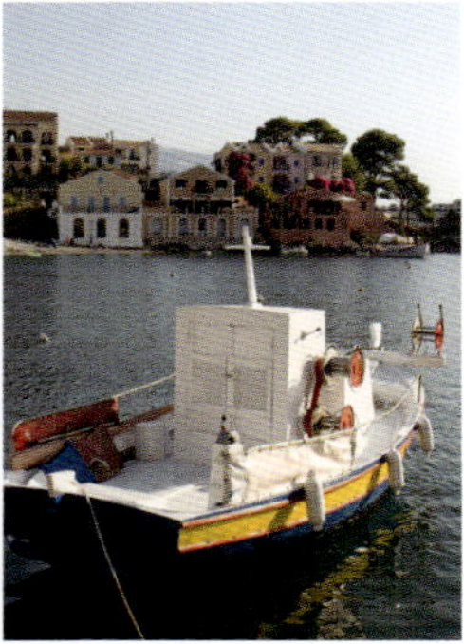

Exposing for both the highlights on the boat and for the sky has left the remainder of this image looking quite dark (far left). However, exposing for the background (center) has resulted in blown highlights in the sky and the boat, which can't be recovered on your computer.

Holding the highlights at least gives you the chance to brighten the shadow regions on a computer later (left).

Expose to the Right

Although superficially this may sound similar to the previous tip, there is a subtle and important difference. The "right," of course, refers to the right-hand side of the histogram, the highlight area. So why should we want the histogram to show a lot of brightly exposed pixels? Aren't we trying to make sure highlights aren't blown? Wouldn't it be safer to expose to the left, or underexpose? Well, although it might be safer, if undertaken with care—making sure that highlights aren't actually blown, or clipped at the right-hand edge of the histogram—exposing to the right, or slightly overexposing, improves the signal-to-noise ratio (SNR) in the shadow regions. The result is less noise in the darker tones—where it is usually most apparent—when the image is later edited on computer.

Exposing to the right works best for images with a lot of shadow or mid-dark tones and, as previously indicated, only if you intend to edit them. Again, you'll reap greater benefits shooting Raw files, which as 12-bit or even 14-bit files, contain more color information. Open the Raw file in your Raw conversion program and adjust the brightness levels so that the histogram is spread more evenly across the tones before opening the file in your software-editing program. The image will now look less overexposed, without introducing noise in the shadow regions.

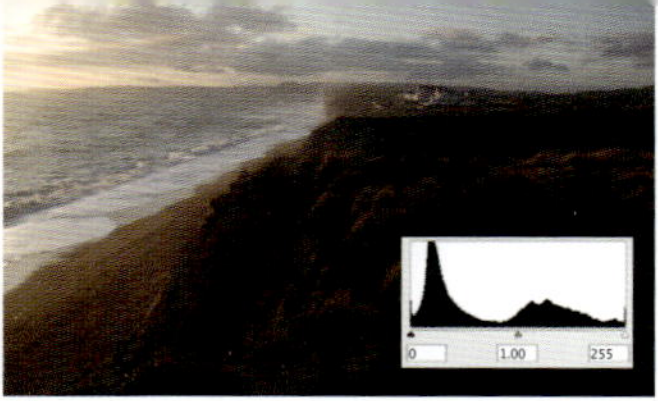

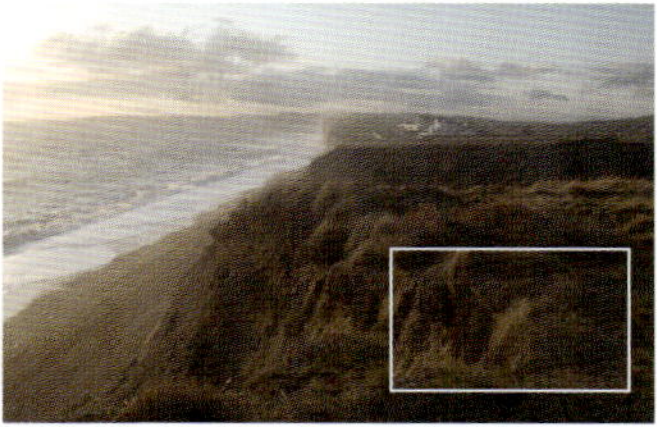

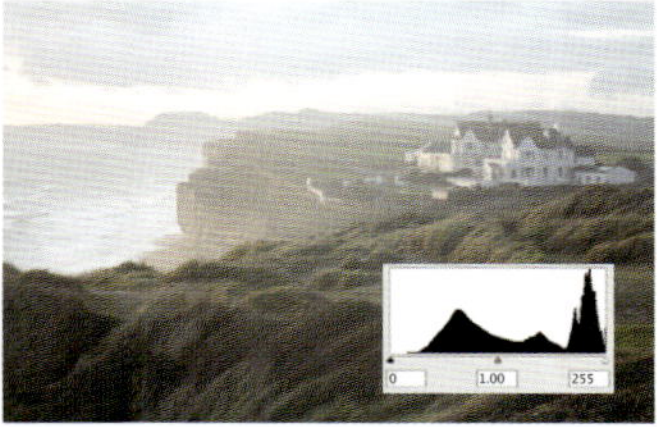

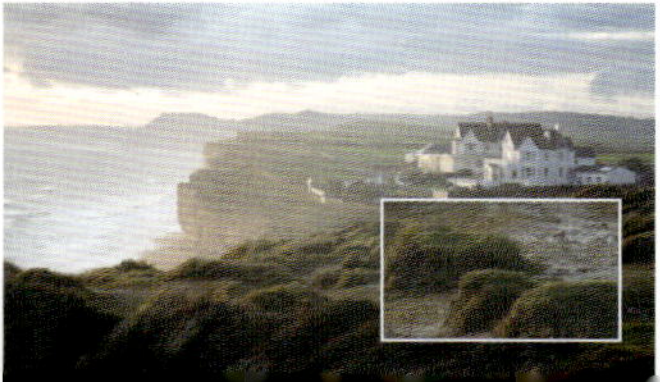

This sequence of shots and accompanying histograms illustrates how, if you're careful to avoid clipping highlights, exposing to the right can result in better signal-to-noise ratio in shadow areas. The first shot shows a good spread of tones, but with a large shadow area in the foreground. When trying to lighten this area in post-production, noise is introduced and the colors become muddy. In the second shot, the image has been deliberately overexposed slightly, while still holding the highlights. Now, when the image is amended in post-production to balance the tones, far less noise is introduced into the foreground shadow region, and the colors are more accurately rendered.

Exposure and Post-production

Of course, we should always strive to get the best possible exposure in-camera at all times. But often there will be occasions when, due to the high dynamic range of the scene we want to capture, we should remember what is achievable on a computer during post-production using image-editing software.

Perhaps the most common scenario is trying to expose for a bright sky without underexposing the ground beneath. It's to counter this exact situation that photographers have been using neutral density graduated filters that fit on the end of the lens. The filter effectively reduces the brightness in the sky, and because it graduates to clear glass, the ground remains unaffected. The overall result is to balance the exposure. However, a similar result can be achieved using software.

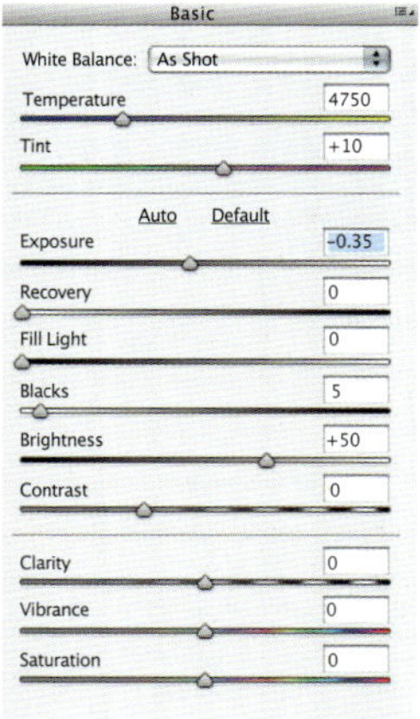

If you shoot Raw, you can set the exposure for the sky in your Raw conversion software and save one version of the image. Open the Raw file again, set the exposure for the ground, and save another version. You can then combine both versions to create a perfectly exposed image.

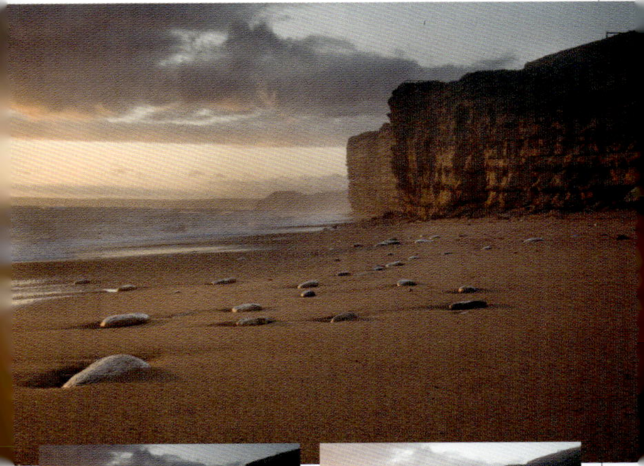

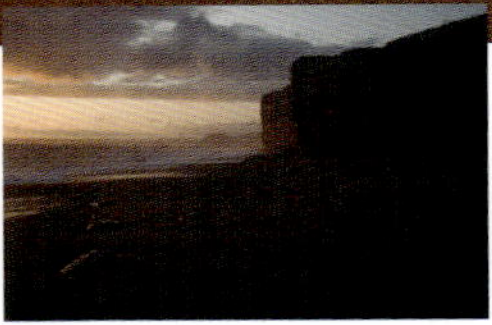

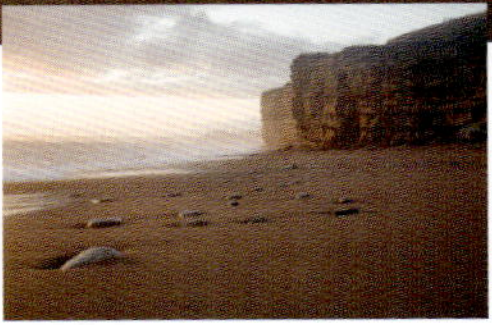

The situation all photographers are familiar with. Exposing for the sky results in underexposed foreground (above left), while exposing for the land results in an overexposed sky (above right). Taking two or more exposures and combining them on computer gets the desired final result (top). For the best results, place the camera on a tripod and bracket to obtain the exposures you need. Using continuous shooting mode will mean the exposures are taken in very quick succession, overcoming any alignment problems with slow-moving elements.

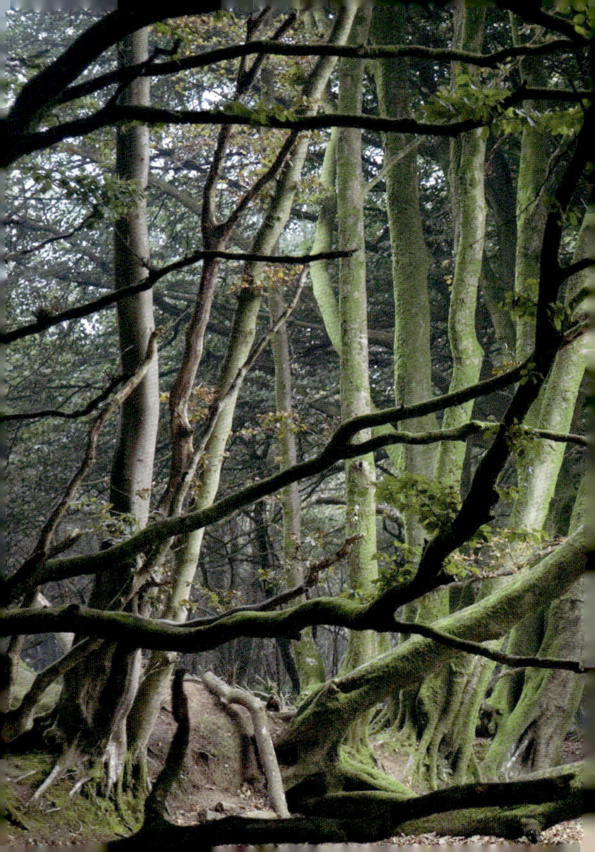

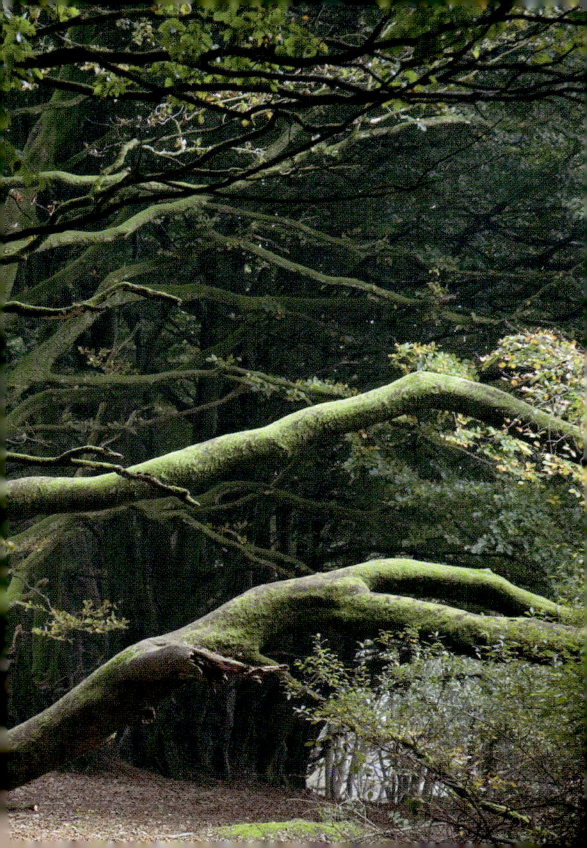

Using Built-in Flash

Most digital SLRs have a built-in, or pop-up flash. Naturally, such a small flash unit cannot possibly compare with the much larger and more powerful detachable flash guns that are available for all makes of digital SLR, however, having some form of permanently accessible flash does have some advantages.

When your camera is set to one of the subject exposure modes, (except, perhaps Landscape, Sports, or No Flash modes) the flash will automatically pop-up and fire if the camera detects a low-light scene or back-lit subject. The effective range of the flash increases with higher ISO settings (due to increased sensitivity) and larger apertures (smaller number).

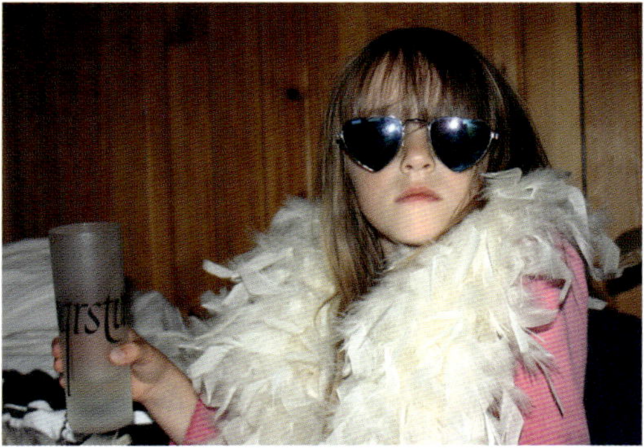

A typical pop-up flash situation. Due to poor lighting, the pop-up flash has fired. The result is harsh, frontal lighting, and the flash is unattractively reflected in the sunglasses; but at least a record of the occasion was made possible.

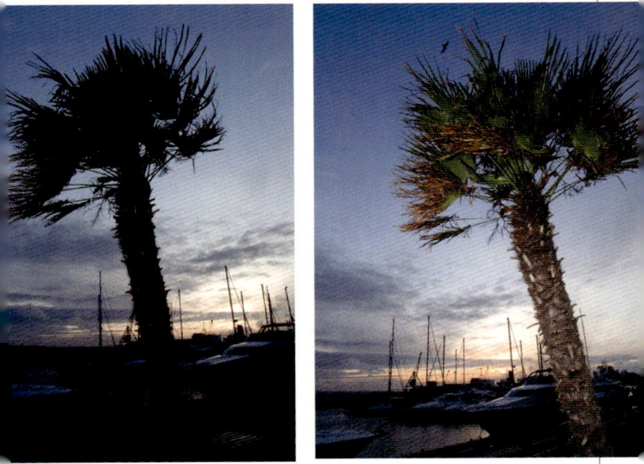

Fill-in flash completely transforms this shot of a tree. Lit by semi-diffused backlight alone, the tree is in shadow and the whole image lacks any impact, but flash, combined with daylight, creates a more striking shot of the tree.

Fill-in flash

Earlier we discussed how the camera would call on the built-in flash if it detected a back-lit subject. In such situations, the overall light levels may not necessarily warrant an additional light source, but because the subject is strongly lit from behind the camera will meter for the bright background and the subject will be underexposed. To prevent this, the camera uses the built-in flash to balance out the differences in the light behind the subject and the light coming off the subject.

Other fill-in situations

Fill-in flash can be useful even if the subject isn't necessarily strongly back-lit. In cases where direct sunlight, usually when the sun is overhead, casts unflattering shadows across the subject's face, a small amount of fill-in flash can lighten the shadows to make them appear less prominent.

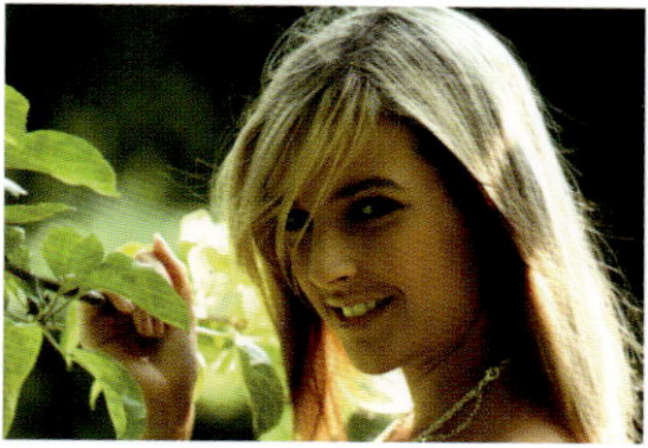

Fill-in flash can lighten deep shadows when the daylight is very contrasty.

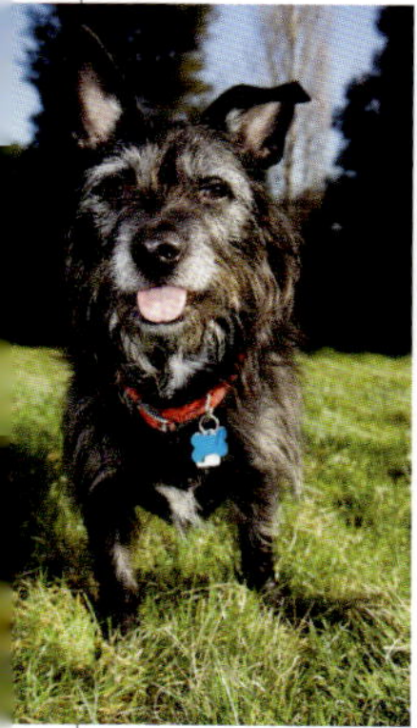

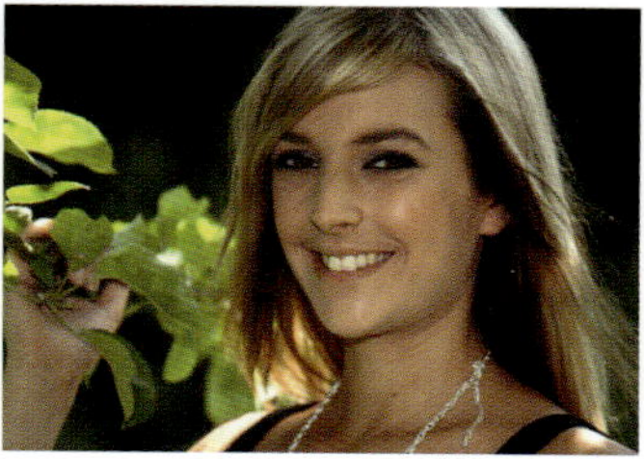

Using a small amount of fill-in flash when the sun is bright and casting strong shadows on the subject's face can help to create more even tones. Getting just the right amount of flash takes a bit of practice.

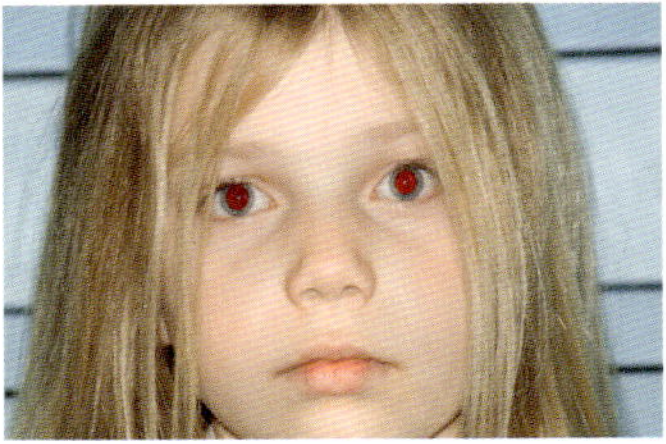

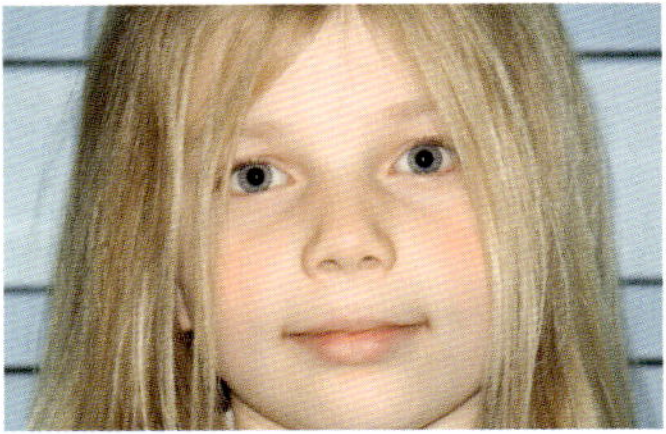

These two shots were taken with a 200mm telephoto setting in almost complete darkness. Without red-eye reduction the girl's irises are totally dilated and the red-eye is easily noticeable. Using red-eye reduction has removed the red-eye effect.

Red-eye reduction

One of the recurring problems when using on-camera flash to photograph people is "red-eye." This is caused by the close proximity of the flash to the lens, so that when the flash fires the light shines directly into the subject's eyes, bounces off the retina, and lights the red blood vessels. Most digital SLRs have a red-eye reduction lamp that pulses when the shutter button is pressed halfway. This encourages the subject's irises, which are wide in low-light conditions, to shrink, so letting less light through to the back of the eye. Get as close as possible to your subject, and ask them to look directly into the lamp as it flashes to get the best results.

Flash Exposure Compensation

In the semi-manual and manual exposure modes, it's possible to adjust the brightness of the flash. It works in much the same way as normal exposure compensation (see pages 48-49), and is, unsurprisingly, called Flash Exposure Compensation. Push the Flash Exposure Compensation button, or select the control via the camera's menu, depending on your specific model. In the viewfinder or on the LCD panel on the top of the camera, you'll find a scale bar, running from –2 to + 2, with the Flash Exposure Compensation symbol above it. Using the Quick Control Dial or buttons on the back of the camera you can increase or decrease the flash output, and the scale bar will indicate the setting.

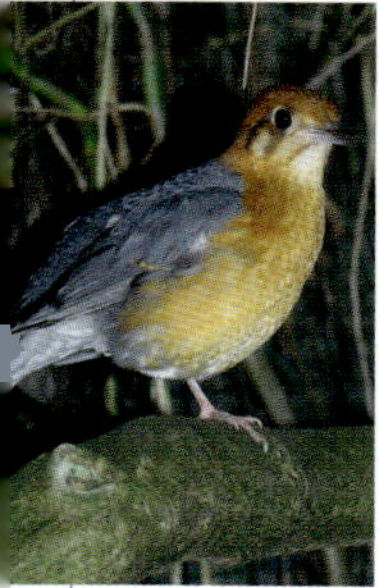

NO FLASH COMPENSATION

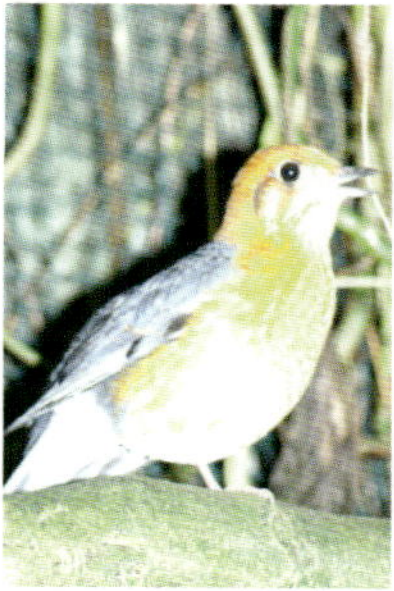

FLASH COMPENSATION +2

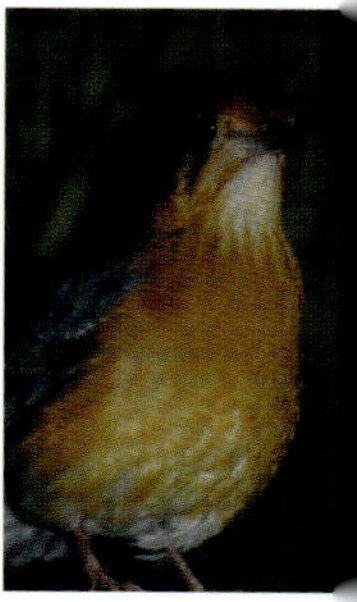

FLASH COMPENSATION –1

While it's possible to increase and decrease the strength of the flash with flash exposure compensation, in practice, with built-in flash at least, the function is used more often to reduce the output in order to produce less harshly lit results.

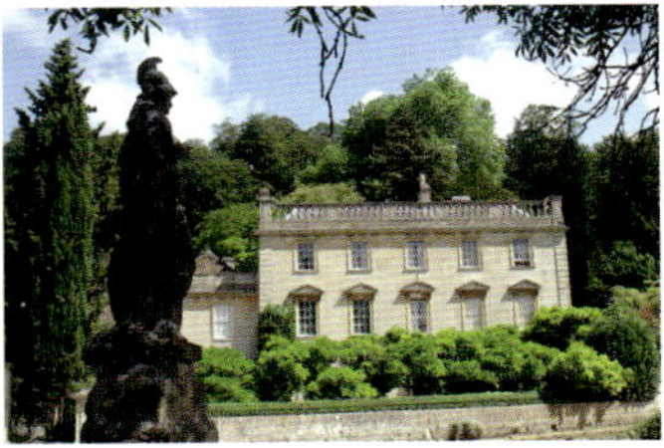

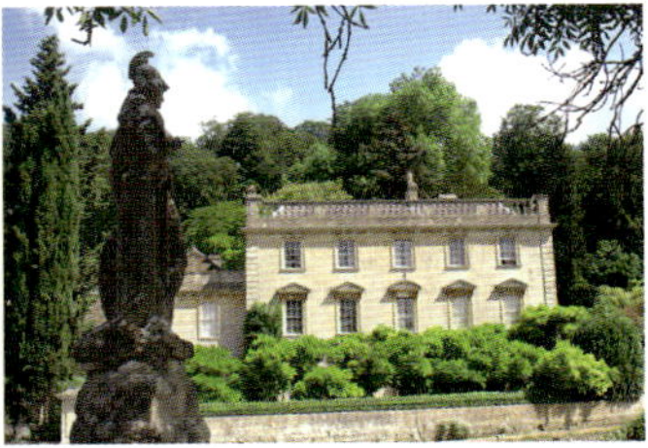

Without fill-in flash (top) the statue is almost black. By registering a small amount of flash, using FE Lock to maintain the reading and then recomposing the shot, a much more satisfactory result is reached.

FE (Flash Exposure) Lock

Flash Exposure Lock is very similar to standard AE (auto exposure) Lock (see pages 50-51). You can use it to obtain the correct exposure for a subject that you wish to place off-center. Activate the pop-up flash by pressing the appropriate button. Focus on the subject and press the AE Lock button on the back of the camera. The flash will fire and the camera will register and store the correct flash exposure for the subject. You can now recompose the shot and fire the shutter. Although the subject is no longer in the center of the frame, the camera will use the flash output recorded earlier to light the subject accurately.

Detachable flash units

All digital SLRs can be fitted with a detachable flash unit. These are attached to the camera via the connection found on the top of the camera, commonly referred to as the "hot shoe." If you find yourself having to use the built-in flash on a regular basis it may be worth investing in such a detachable flash gun, as you'll very quickly reap the benefits of having a more powerful and flexible source of flash.

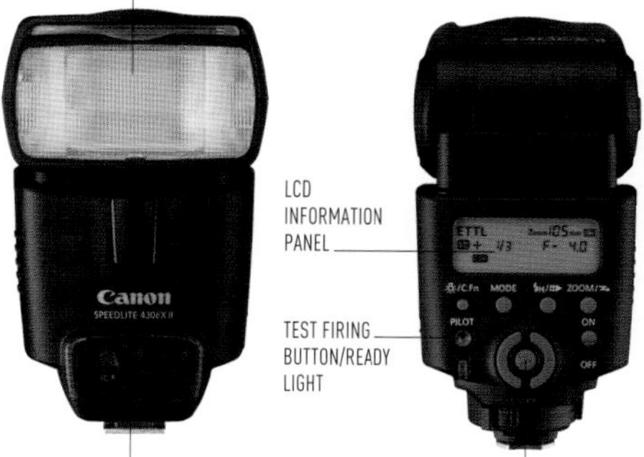

Canon's 430EX II Speedlite is compatible with all Canon digital SLRs. Apart from providing a more powerful light source, and therefore capable of illuminating much further than a built-in flash, it has a whole range of features that will help you get much more naturalistic shots at night and in low light.

Bounce flash

One of the greatest benefits of using a detachable flash unit is that with most models the flash heads are designed to tilt and swivel. This may sound somewhat underwhelming, but having the ability to direct the flash away from the subject can have an enormous effect on the final image.

The idea is to bounce the flash off a large light-colored surface, such as a ceiling or wall. The reflected light, coming from a much larger area (a ceiling as opposed to a flash head) is much more diffused, resulting in a softer, more realistic shot.

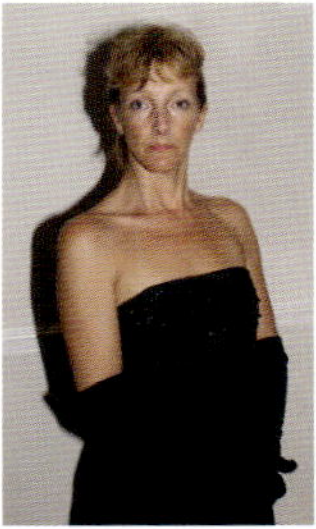

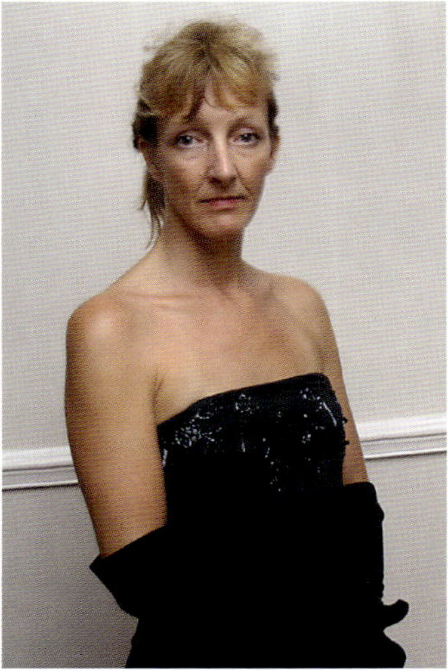

With the camera's built-in flash, exposure is managed automatically, but harsh light creates hard shadows and over bright highlights (above). With flash bounced off the ceiling (right), the portrait no longer has the "look" of a picture taken with flash.

Slow-sync flash

Slow-speed flash synchronization, or slow-sync for short, is traditionally used for night portraits, when you want the background to have the same exposure as the subject. With the camera set in Aperture priority (see page 43) and the flash ready to fire, compose the shot and press the shutter button. The flash will fire and automatically expose the subject, but the camera will then continue to expose for the much darker background. When using slow-sync flash in this way it's important that the camera is firmly supported or else the background will blur due to the longer shutter speed.

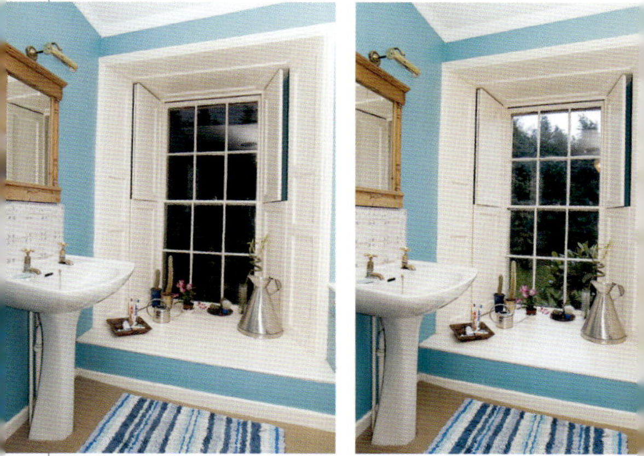

A tripod and long exposure were needed in order to see through the bathroom window in this slow-sync flash shot.

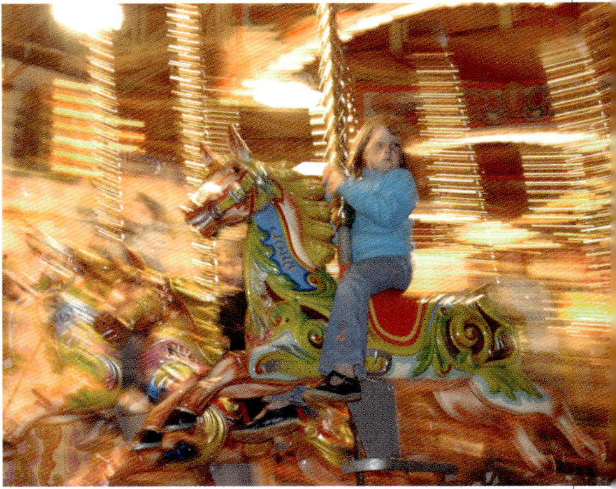

In this energetic shot, a relatively slow shutter speed causes the motion-blur, which is clearly visible in the light trails. The girl, however, is lit by the momentary flash so doesn't appear blurred. The effect is dramatic.

Creative slow-sync

Although slow-sync is traditionally used to balance foreground and background exposures, it can also be used in a creative way. When used with moving objects in the background, the extended shutter speed will cause everything but the subject, whose movement is frozen by the brief light from the flash, to become blurred. The result is an eye-catching combination of sharp subject and blurred background.

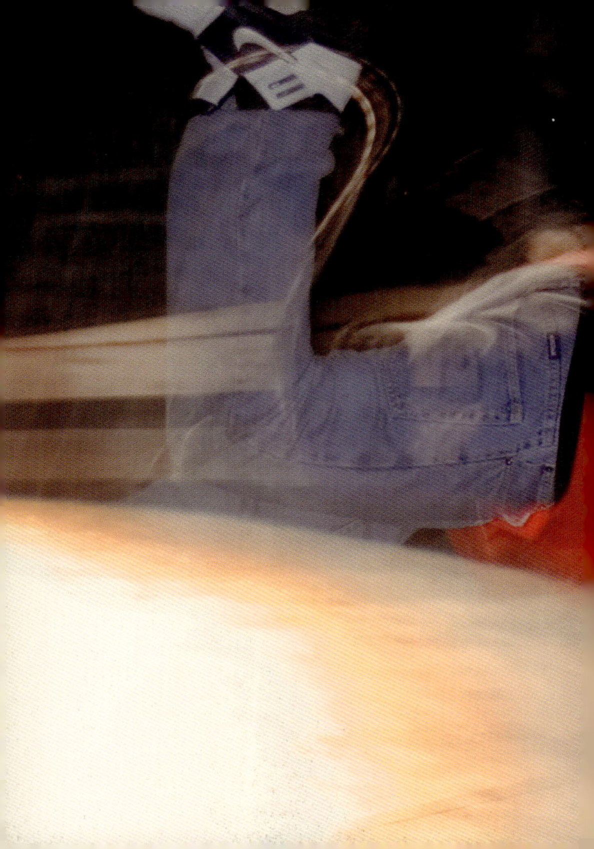

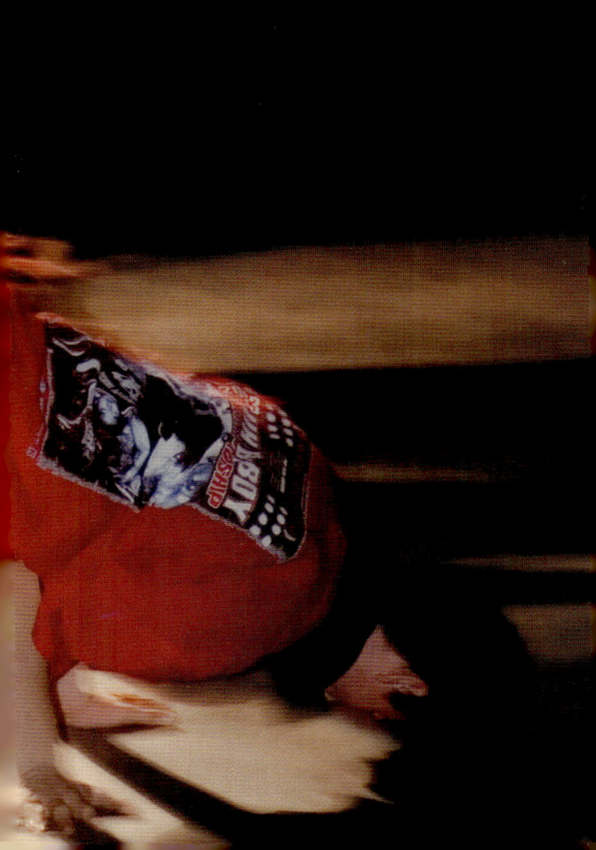

Rear-curtain sync

While slow-sync can produce dramatic low-light results, it can also lead to some rather bizarre and unwanted side-effects in certain situations. If the object you're photographing is moving across the frame in a straight line, and if the exposure is sufficiently long, the blurred part of the image appears to overtake the frozen part, creating an unnatural-looking result. This is because, with standard slow-sync the flash fires at the beginning of the exposure, so the object is frozen at the beginning of the long exposure. Any light trails, therefore, appear in front of the object as they are captured throughout the length of the exposure. To prevent this, most digital SLRs have a rear-curtain (or 2nd-curtain) sync option, which will fire the flash at the end of the exposure rather than at the beginning. The option can be accessed via the camera's menu.

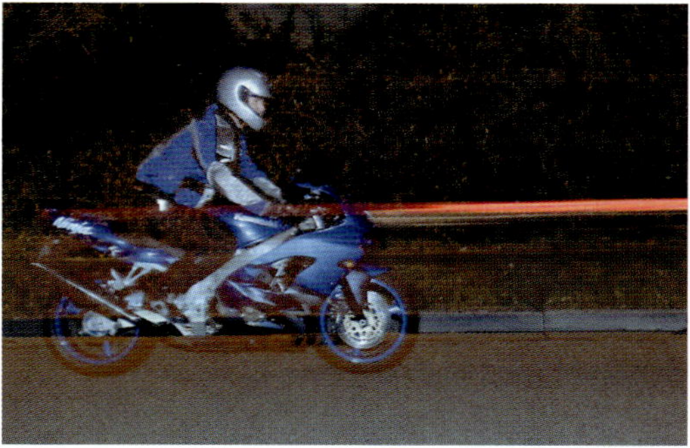

The light trails appear in front of the bike, beacuse of the standard slow-sync, or 1st-curtain sync. An interesting effect, but not quite the desired result.

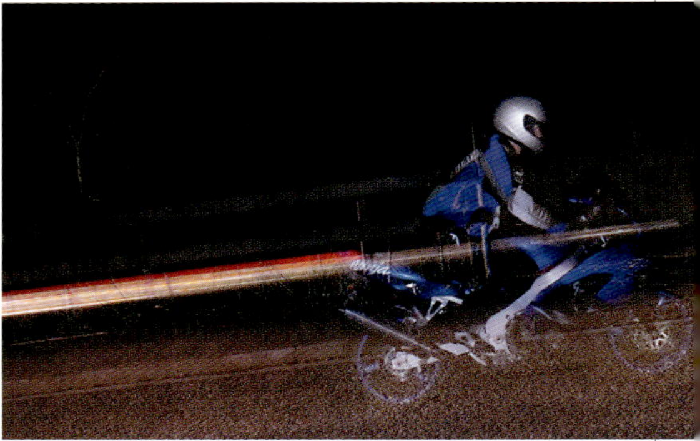

The effect as it was originally envisaged. By using the camera's rear-curtain, or 2nd-curtain sync facility, the flash has fired at the end of the exposure, freezing the bike at the end of the light trails.

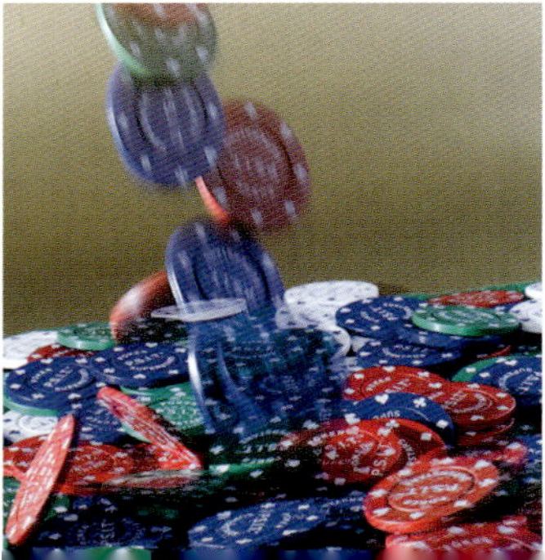

In this shot of poker chips, a slow shutter speed of 2 sec was used with a brief burst of flash. Both 1st- and 2nd-curtain sync were used to see which worked the best. As the blur created was only slight, the difference between the two was unimportant in the end. This is the version taken using 2nd-curtain sync.

Glossary

AE Abbreviation of automatic exposure.

AEL (Automatic Exposure Lock) A push-button control that lets you choose which part of the scene the camera takes its meter reading from, and then lock this setting while the image is reframed.

AF Abbreviation of autofocus.

Ambient light The existing light in the scene, excluding any light source added by the photographer.

Angle of view A measurement of how much a lens can see of a scene from a particular position, usually measured in degrees. The longer the focal length of the lens, the smaller the angle of view. Zoom lenses have adjustable angles of view.

Aperture The opening in the lens that restricts how much light reaches the image sensor. In all but the most basic cameras, the size of the aperture is adjustable. The aperture setting used has an important role to play in both exposure and depth of field.

Aperture priority Semi-automatic exposure system, where the aperture is set by the photographer, and the shutter speed is then set by the camera to suit the light level reading taken by the camera's own meter.

Autofocus A system in which the lens is adjusted automatically by the camera to bring the designated part of the image into sharp focus.

AWB (Automatic White Balance) System that automatically adjusts the color of the recorded picture so that it looks normal to the human eye.

B Abbreviation of bulb. A shutter speed setting on a camera that allows you to keep the shutter open for as long as the shutter release is held down. Used for long exposures that last for seconds or minutes.

Back-lighting Light source that is on the far side of the subject, in relation to the camera.

Bounce flash Indirect flash lighting technique, where the flash gun is angled to bounce off a wall, ceiling, or other reflector. This scatters the illumination, creating a softer lighting effect.

Bracketing System for increasing the chances of getting the right exposure by taking a sequence of pictures with a slightly different exposure setting for each.

Cable release Mechanical or electronic device for firing a camera from a short distance away. Often used as a way to minimize vibration when using a slow shutter speed and a camera support, such as a tripod.

Camera shake Blurring of the image caused by movement of the camera during the exposure. Handheld cameras are prone to camera shake, and a fast shutter speed needs to be used to eliminate the problem.

Center-weighted Type of built-in metering system, provided as an option on some cameras. Center-weighted meters measure light intensity across the entire image area, but bias the average in favor of light taken toward the center of the frame. The system is not foolproof; however, it is easier to predict when it will make an inappropriate reading than more sophisticated metering systems.

Circular polarizer Type of polarizing filter. Circular polarizers can be used with modern cameras without interfering with the operation of exposure metering and autofocus systems, unlike older and cheaper linear polarizers.

Color temperature Measurement of the color of light, usually expressed in degrees Kelvin. The human eye adjusts automatically for color temperature much of the time without us realizing; digital cameras can make electronic adjustments using

their white balance systems to mimic the eye and brain.

Continuous autofocus AF setting where the focus is constantly adjusted until the shutter is actually fired. Useful for moving subjects, where it would be unhelpful for the focus distance to be locked as soon as initially found.

Depth of field A measure of how much of a picture is in focus, from the nearest point in the scene to the camera that looks sharp, to the furthermost point that looks sharp. Depth of field is dependent on the aperture used, the distance that the lens is focused at, and the focal length of the lens.

Depth of field preview Device found on some digital SLRs that enables you to see the viewfinder image at the actual aperture you will be using for the exposure. This gives a visual indication as to how much depth of field there is, and which parts of the resulting picture will be sharp or blurred. This is necessary, as the viewfinder normally only shows the image as it would appear if the widest aperture available were used.

Diaphragm Another term for the aperture. The adjustable blades that regulate how much light enters the lens.

Differential focusing Using depth of field to make sure that one element in the picture is sharp, while others are as out of focus as possible.

Dynamic range A measure of the range of image densities that can be recorded by a device, from its brightest white to its darkest black.

EV (Exposure Value) Scale used to denote the exposure required without the need to specify either shutter speed or aperture. A particular Ev setting has its own set pairs of possible shutter speed and aperture. Exposure values are often quoted in combination with an ISO speed to denote a specific light level.

Evaluative metering Metering system used on many cameras where light readings are taken from a

number of different areas, or zones, across the image. These are then compared to data programmed into the camera, so it can work out an appropriate exposure setting. Information from the multipoint autofocus system is also used, to ascertain the likely position of the subject. This "intelligent" metering system can avoid many of the failings of simpler exposure metering systems. However, it is impossible to second-guess, so it can be difficult to predict the occasions where it will get the exposure wrong. Also known as matrix metering.

Exposure Total amount of light used to create an image.

Exposure compensation A control for manually overriding the built-in exposure meter of a camera to provide more or less light to the sensor.

f number The aperture setting. The number is the focal length of the lens divided by the diameter of the aperture; because of this, larger f numbers represent smaller aperture sizes. f numbers are used so that exposure settings for a particular scene can be expressed without having to know the focal length actually used.

Focal length Optical term describing the distance between the optical center of a lens and its focal point. In practice, the focal length is a measure of the magnification and angle of view of a given lens or zoom setting. It is usually measured in millimeters.

f stop See f number.

Fast ISO setting An ISO setting that makes the sensor more sensitive to light than usual, and thus requires less exposure than usual. Fast settings are useful in low light situations where long shutter speeds are not suitable. A drawback is that grain-like noise within the image becomes more pronounced as the ISO speed is increased. See ISO.

Fast lens A lens that has a wider maximum aperture than is usual for that

particular focal length or zoom range. Fast lenses are not only useful in low light; they can be invaluable for throwing backgrounds out of focus to a greater extent than usual.

Fast shutter speed Relative term for an exposure that is shorter than average, usually set to avoid the blur that would otherwise be created by subject movement.

Frontal lighting Lighting directed toward the subject, and therefore positioned behind, or level, with the camera.

Gray card Card with an 18% gray tint that is used for exposure metering. A meter reading taken from the surface of the card, rather from the subject, can be used to measure the ambient light levels. This is useful when photographing non-average scenes—such as those that are mostly black—which would otherwise mislead the meter.

Grayscale A digital black and white image made up of 256 shades of gray tone.

Highlight The brightest areas of an image—the white areas in a picture.

Histogram Graph used as a way of depicting the brightness, tonal range, and contrast of an image during digital manipulation. Also used as a way of evaluating exposure by some cameras.

Hyperfocal distance The shortest distance at which a lens can be focused so that depth of field stretches to infinity for a given aperture and focal length. When focused at the hyperfocal length, depth of field will stretch from exactly half the hyperfocal distance to infinity.

Inverse square law Property of light where the intensity of light decreases in proportion to the square of the distance from its source. Because the sun is so far away, this has no noticeable influence with natural light. However, it has a significant effect over the

characteristics and usable range of flash, and other artificial light sources.

Manual exposure Exposure mode where both shutter speed and aperture are set by the photographer.

Matrix metering See Evaluative metering.

Metered manual Exposure mode where, although shutter speed and aperture are set manually by the user, information as to their suitability is provided by the camera's own metering system.

Neutral density (ND) Optical or electronic filter that reduces the amount of light reaching the image sensor equally across the entire field of view. It permits longer shutter speeds or wider apertures than would otherwise be possible in the lighting conditions.

Partial metering Type of metering system where the exposure reading is taken from a small area in the center of the field of view. Similar to spot metering, but the reading is taken from a larger area of the image.

Polarizer A filter that transmits only light vibrating in one plane. It can be used to deepen the color of part of a picture, such as the sky. It can also be used to eliminate or reduce reflections on non-metallic surfaces, such as water or glass. It must be rotated in front of the lens until you achieve the desired effect. See circular polarizer.

Program exposure Any exposure mode where the camera sets both aperture and shutter speed automatically.

Program shift Program exposure mode where the camera sets the shutter speed and aperture automatically, but the photographer has the option of altering the bias between the two readings to set a preferred shutter speed or aperture without changing the overall exposure.

Raw A native file format offered by some digital cameras. Image data is stored in a semi-processed state

and must be fully processed on a computer. Enables exposure compensation and color balance to be altered after camera exposure, and typically provides a 48-bit color depth option.

Rear curtain sync Flash feature found on some digital SLRs and flashguns that synchronizes the flash output when the second shutter curtain is about to close. Usually, the flash fires at the point where the first shutter is fully open. The facility gives more natural-looking images when using flash in conjunction with slow shutter speeds.

Rim lighting Back-lighting where the edges of the subject are illuminated in such a way to create a halo-like effect.

Second curtain sync Alternative term for rear curtain sync.

Self-timer Camera facility that incorporates a delay between the pressing of the trigger and the beginning of the exposure. Traditionally used to enable the photographer to appear in the shot. But it can also be useful as as a way of minimizing vibration when using a slow shutter speed with some form of camera support.

Shutter priority Semi-automatic exposure mode where the shutter speed is set by the photographer, and the aperture is then set by the camera to suit the metered light readings taken by the camera.

Skylight filter A UV and warm-up filter combined; sometimes left permanently attached to a lens as a way of protecting the front element from being scratched.

Slow sync flash Technique where a slow shutter speed is used in conjunction with flash. The flash usually provides the main source of illumination, but the ambient light creates a secondary exposure that can be useful in suggesting movement, or for providing detail in a background that

would otherwise have looked unnaturally dark.

Spot meter Exposure metering system where a meter reading is taken from a very small area in the center of the frame.

Stop A unit of exposure. Changing exposure by a single stop is equivalent to doubling or halving the amount of light reaching the image sensor. The distance between each of the standard aperture settings (f2.8, f4, f 5.6, f 8, etc) is a full stop.

Stop down To close down the aperture.

Sync speed The fastest shutter speed that can be set on a camera that enables synchronization with the flash. See flash synchronization.

TTL (Through The Lens) metering Exposure system where the intensity of light is measured through the main camera lens.

Tv (Time Value) abbreviation used for shutter priority on some cameras.

UV filter Optical filter that absorbs ultraviolet (UV) radiation. Can be used to improve visibility and quality in mountain and maritime landscapes.

Vignetting Darkening of the corners of an image, normally due to lens falloff. Can be corrected in software.

White balance Digital camera system that sets the color temperature for the scene being photographed. This can be set automatically, with the system attempting to set the color so that it looks normal to the human eye. Many cameras also offer manual white balance settings.

Zoom A lens with a variable angle of view.

Index

A

B

C

D

E